THE *NEW* PHOTOGRAPHY

A MODERN GUIDEBOOK TO BETTER PHOTOGRAPHY

TEXT AND PHOTOGRAPHY BY BRADLEY SMITH

A Gemini Smith Book  Revised Edition © 1977

Published simultaneously in the United States and Canada by Playboy Press, Chicago, Illinois. Printed in the United States of America.

First Edition
Playboy and Rabbit Head design are trademarks of Playboy, 919 North Michigan Avenue, Chicago, Illinois 60611 (U.S.A.). Reg. U.S. Pat. Off., marca registrada, marque déposée.

Library of Congress Catalog No. 75-24266
ISBN No. 87223-435-5
Simon & Schuster No. 16852

P̶P
PLAYBOY PRESS

THE *NEW* PHOTOGRAPHY

TABLE OF CONTENTS

Giraffes greeting was made with a 200mm telephoto lens. Background is over-exposed to bring out the interesting skin pattern in these reticulated types.

Frontispiece
An abstract nude made with a 5 prism lens. When used over a conventional lens, they can be manipulated to obtain a wide variety of multiple images.

Unearthly effect is given in this study of Africa's Nile River in the late afternoon by using a fog filter. The sun is high and behind cloud cover.

THE *NEW* PHOTOGRAPHY

INTRODUCTION

The new cameras (including miniature and sub-miniature sizes), the new films, lenses, shutters, electronic exposure controls, all combine to make it easier to take good pictures. You will learn in this guidebook where photography is today. You will learn how, with modern cameras, films and lenses currently available, you can be relatively sure of obtaining an image when you press the release. You will learn something of the past, of how today's photography came to be. You will see examples among the photographs illustrating the book that show the different viewpoints and different styles of photography. But important questions still remain and only you can answer them.

You are standing on the edge of a cliff watching a beautiful sunset; you are walking along a street in New York and stop in front of the Paul Manship sculpture at Rockefeller Center; you are watching a two-year-old play with a puppy; you are at the circus or at an amateur theatrical event, a football game—you have your camera and you look at each of these scenes through the viewfinder. Now is the time to ask yourself a most important question that is going to affect your life with a camera: Why take the picture? You may even have to ask yourself this question twice before you decide whether or not to press the shutter release. Why take the picture? What are you going to do with it? Does it have the evidence of a color slide that you want to project later? Is the picture going to make an effective enlargement for your wall or your album? Does this scene have some importance or relation to your life style? Do you really want to see this picture again—ever? You will take better pictures, though fewer, if you ask yourself these questions before you press the release.

I am suggesting that the photographer, amateur or professional, needs to be selective. It is easy enough to point the camera and press the button at random, but what a waste! Instead of uselessly burning up the film, you can use it to take a picture that will be of some permanent value to you or to others.

Deciding whether the picture should be taken or not is the beginning of photographic experience. The painter does not try to reproduce everything that he sees, but rather tries to extract meaning from scenes that he understands. Photography contains within it the essence of reality. The camera does record what it sees. But you are in charge of what it sees and you can add importance to the scene before you by your evaluation of its meaning to you.

Do not let the brilliance of the sunset blind you to the fact that there are sunsets every day, all interesting in one way or another. But do you want hundreds of sunsets in your file? Do not allow the "cute" or corny elements of the child and dog to affect your judgment—select not only the scenes but the moments that you want to preserve.

When you asked yourself whether or not to take the picture, you were making a personal value judgment; but such decisions involve an additional factor, which I will call *photographic economy.* One picture of a church interior or a waterfall may mean a great deal to you. But 10 pictures like either of these reduce the value of your one picture and increase film and processing costs. Many groups of people, including many Asians, believe that a picture loses value when it is duplicated too many times or when too many eyes view the original. In all primitive societies, the most sacred object within the tribe has always been hidden from general view. I am not suggesting that you not show the picture that you do take widely. But I am suggesting that the picture should represent some effort, some decision on your part as a photographer.

The new photographic techniques allow you to communicate more easily. Technical advances, which are hidden inside the new cameras and which need not really concern you, allow you to record almost anything that comes before your eyes. This makes your responsibility greater. Your eye can therefore select, even distort or change shape, color, texture, yet you must know something of what you want in your final picture. You must see it not only in your eye but in your mind.

That this book deals with the new photography, the photography of today, does not imply that it excludes the old ways in photography. What is new is not enough. All modern photography rests on a solid base of 125 years of aesthetic and scientific progress. Out of the historic images of the past have come those of the present.

Today we live in a photographic maze of superlatives. New cameras have electric eyes, computerized mechanisms and electric brains. Complete light-making machines are available. An extension of your eye can be carried around in your pocket. There is an automatic system that guarantees perfect flash exposures. And one supplier offers a portable ceiling as part of a complete artificial light-making machine. There are super multi-coated short focal length and long focal length lenses that allow you to photograph anything from a flea's antenna to craters on the moon.

In this book we will try to find a way through the confusion of cameras, lenses, filters, chemicals, studio lights, flash umbrellas, exposure meters, film types and speeds to make it possible for the interested amateur to chart a course that will lead to the pleasures of photography.

There are some things this book will not do. It will not select your camera for you, but it will give you advice on how to select one intelligently. It will not tell you which film to use or when to use it, but it will tell you enough about films so you can make a knowledgeable choice. It will not tell you how to build a darkroom or how to develop film, but it will supply guidelines allowing you to decide whether or not you want a darkroom and want to develop and print your own film (considering the disadvantages) or have experts do it for you.

Its emphasis is on the art of photography rather than the science of photography for the new photography is far more than a matter of scientific achievement. What began as a scientific marvel and a magic trick has turned out to be much more than an important mechanical tool. Photography has not only documented the world we live in, but has interpreted and revealed it as well—sometimes it has created a world of its own. What began as a scattering of specialists who recorded the physical appearance of our ancestors in small brown-tone pictures called daguerreotypes has become a multitude of adventurers, explorers, inventors, scientists, manufacturers and, perhaps not surprisingly, artists. Not artists with pen, paper, brush and paints, but humble, seeking humans of every age recording their preferences with a small black box with a lens and sensitized film.

The photographs in this book are part of my life as a photographer. My camera has taken me on assignments to almost every country in the world. I have photographed the great, the near great and the not so great. My subjects have included presidents, entrepreneurs, motion picture actors and actresses, theatrical celebrities, writers, artists, Stone Age Indians, regions of plenty and areas of famine. To me photography has been an education as well as a craft. It taught me how to use my eyes and hands for pleasure and for profit.

To photograph the trail of Lewis and Clark, I traveled over the route they took from the Mississippi River, across the wide Missouri, over the mountains and, by canoe, down the waters of the Clearwater, the Snake and the Columbia Rivers to the Pacific. I shared the feeling of Meriwether Lewis at the end of that journey when, upon viewing the Pacific Ocean, he said, "O! What joy." I, too, experienced a great sense of accomplishment.

The picture of Helen Keller was taken as part of a series of photographs to illustrate an article called *The World through Three Senses.* She could only touch, taste and smell. As preparation I spent an afternoon blindfolded trying to get some idea of how it might feel to be blind. But when I went to photograph Miss Keller, she acted as though she could see as well as I. She had learned the exact location of everything within her house, the distance from tree to tree and from flower bush to shrub in her garden, and had so developed her sense of touch that I got the impression she was moving with radar sensors extended.

Harry Truman was looking for a photographer to illustrate a series of articles which would describe how it felt to be ex-president of the U.S. The articles, and a subsequent book, were to be called *Mr. Citizen*. His editors sent him a sampling of pictures by different photographers along with my pictures of Helen Keller. He said he liked the "feel" of them and I was invited to Independence where I spent each day from dawn until about 10 P.M. documenting how Harry Truman lived. His favorite picture from that series appears in this book.

Both Helen Keller and Harry Truman had one thing in common with the religious political leader Mohandas Gandhi. They were up and going about their daily activities before sunrise. This meant I had to be on location, with my cameras loaded and ready to shoot, by 5 A.M. But it was worth it. The early morning pictures in all three instances proved to be the best.

I feel I have been fortunate in not being typed as a portrait photographer, nature photographer, sports photographer or fashion photographer. I have worked in all those fields. Which do I like best? For the most part, I enjoy changing from one kind of photography to another. Some days I will feel like a documentarian, others like a portraitist and hopefully, on still other days, I'll want to experiment with abstract ideas, nudes or nature. Photography has so broad a base—there are so many different ways to see the world and everything in it—that you can find your own specialty and still be able to go from one type of image to another.

1
GETTING STARTED

So you've never been able to copy that picture in the advertisements that say "learn how to draw (or paint) and make your fortune," and you've never been able to bring yourself to answer those advertisements that will make you a famous writer after a series of lessons by mail. You learned a long time ago that you were never going to be a great musician. So what's left? Well, you can be a photographer and take interesting pictures. You may even turn out to be an artist with a camera for photography offers creative expression to everyone. You don't have to be able to read music, draw or paint pictures. It isn't necessary that you be able to write, but it does help if you can read and this book, based upon 35 years of professional photography, makes it possible for you to start at the top.

There are actually no intricate formulas to learn, and this is a good time to dispel the ideas that you have to be a chemist in the darkroom, a mathematician with the exposure meter or an expert at optics. Most cameras today are so automated, and the use of film so simple, that you are free to create any kind of picture that appeals to you. As you use the camera, you'll find your sense of design improves. You will be able to compose a picture in your own way after only a few weeks with a camera.

You will find great joy in making permanent images whether they be portraits, sport pictures, scenics, travel, records of joyous occasions with your children, your wife, husband, lover, housemate, friends or animals—the camera affords you all of these possibilities. It affords others too—still lifes or flowers, distinctive architecture, autumn foliage, statues. To all of these forms you can add your own individual, special touch.

Do not be afraid to be an artist. You should develop your own style and, indeed, it is hard to avoid showing some of your personality by the way you take pictures. The freer you feel about posing the model for the portrait or the group or the nude, the more it will reflect your own personality. If you see an unusual angle or curve that you think makes the picture more interesting, if there is a hat or a costume handy that will help to express the personality of the model, use it. To take good pictures, you must become an explorer. The camera will at times be your telescope, at other times your microscope. The world comes under your personal observation. What you see and the way that you see it become the pictures that you create. You may show the model what you want or the model may express himself. It is in your power to make people look the way you want them to look, to show a flower in the light and against a background you select. The camera becomes an extension of your creativity.

Exploring the nude figure is another rewarding way of using your camera. The female nude has been the model of beauty in humans since before the beginning of recorded history. Stone Age artists, painters both good and bad, and photographers ever since the invention of the medium have found working with the nude an ever changing, creative experience.

The opportunities with your camera are endless. But how can you develop and control your instinct to either photograph nothing or everything? There is some voyeurism in everyone which makes them look with interest at objects, scenes and humans and it is easy to learn to see and record the life around you.

An hour with the camera can take your mind away from tensions and allow you to live in a world of your own. Even the casual snapshot can be improved by learning the simple rules outlined in this book. You can take pictures of permanent value, avoiding the errors amateurs continually make. You can find out what kind of camera may be best for you, what type of film, and what area of photography best suits your own personality. You can learn how to keep from wasting film and producing pictures you'll never want to see again.

Photography can help you improve your concept of design and composition, your sense of color and your sense of humor. It can reveal sentiment that you didn't know you had. You can learn to make pictures that will not only please you but also please the people you photograph. No one need remain an amateur. When you pick up your camera and begin to think about photographs, you are on your way to a professional attitude. Your approach is to take the best pictures you can. You may even want to go a step further and use this book as a base for a profitable career in professional photography.

It is fortunate that everyone sees things just a little bit differently. No two points of view are exactly alike. The kind of picture that pleases one person may have no effect, or little effect, on another. So you take charge each time you select a subject to photograph, an angle to photograph it from, and a way of composing the picture in the viewfinder. The camera is only an instrument for recording what you, with your eye and mind, have selected.

The eye can be trained to see many things which you may not have been conscious of seeing before. Try looking carefully at a familiar object near you—perhaps a corner of a room in which there is a lamp. Then, with your hands open, fingers together, thumbs extended and touching, form a square with the top missing. Hold your hands a few inches from your eyes and you will see framed what the camera sees when a wide angle lens is used. Now move your hands out from your eyes about six inches and you get the usual 50-55mm lens view that is standard on most cameras. Compose your picture inside the frame moving your hands with your eyes as you select the best angle. You can move up, down, to the right or to the left, until the composition pleases you. Should you want to know how the picture would look with a telephoto lens, simply move your hands out from your face a foot or more and, as you look through your extended hands, you will see very much what the 135mm lens will record.

Make every effort to see objects and people within a framework. Many pictures can be preframed by using your hands as described above and then looking through the viewfinder of your camera. You may find that the common viewfinder is not necessary after awhile. The picture may turn out to be so uninteresting you won't want to go to the trouble of taking it at all. But remember it is you, with your perception, your insight, who are responsible for the final picture.

Different kinds of photography, just as different kinds of music, appeal to different people. One of the late great photographers, Edward Weston, made magnificent still lifes photographing such ordinary objects as green peppers, bananas, artichokes and flowers. But he put such concentration into the pictures that the resulting images show how he *saw* the green peppers, a point of view strictly his own. He even photographed the forms of artichokes and green peppers in a manner that made them sexually stimulating. Photographs of flowers can be another rewarding type of camera work and most cameras, even the inexpensive ones, can be fitted with a supplementary lens allowing you to do close-ups.

But if still lifes and flowers are not your forte, you may turn to the wide range of other types of photography. The most common is snapshots of friends or family. These need not be ordinary pictures of head and shoulders or full figures of people self-consciously facing the camera. Practice photographing people while they are doing something rather than just posing for you. And, even if they are posing for you, try to get them in some revealing attitude such as playing the piano or the guitar, lying on the grass, leaning against a tree, reading a book. The snapshot may include one or many people but, for it to be effective, it should be a picture that evokes some memories of time and place. It differs greatly from the formal portrait by its very informality and candid quality.

There are many other specialized fields and each of them will be taken up in a chapter devoted to it, such as portraiture, the nude, travel and action photography. Every photographer can expect many failures in his early pictures, but there is no reason to despair. It is rare that the camera fails; it is almost always the photographer behind it. Sometimes the blank picture or the flawed picture can be immediately traced to such simple errors as improper film loading, neglecting to remove the lens cap, battery failure in the automatic camera, moving the camera during the exposure, or neglecting to note that a tree seems to be growing out of the head of the subject or that the complicated background makes the picture a failure. Remember, no one is an artist all of the time; not even the greatest artists always painted great pictures.

It is essential to become completely familiar with your camera, familiar with light, familiar with film. The best way to do this is by trial and error. Take a walk in any direction, even through your home or apartment; any kind of walk can reveal interesting pictures. Use the camera in different light conditions. Try to take pictures that evoke the way you feel, or pictures of people and objects that interest you. Edward Weston once shot a series of widely published pictures of an ordinary toilet because he liked the shape of the porcelain bowl and base. Irving Penn once photographed a series of beat-up cigarette butts and they were exhibited at the Museum of Modern Art. A German photographer created a book of unique photographs showing his wife's bare behind in different well known locations throughout Europe. It was a success, as was a book of photographs devoted entirely to water. There is a famous Japanese book composed entirely of pictures of snow.

The words used to describe different types of photography are the snapshot, the documentary, the candid photograph, the posed picture, the available or natural light photograph, flash pictures, nudes, still lifes, nature and action pictures. Most of these categories overlap one another. But, to make crystal clear what each one means, we will take them up separately.

The snapshot.   The word itself is derived from a hunting term: instead of having time to aim carefully and shoot, the hunter, seeing an animal or a bird, quickly raises his gun and takes a snap shot. Even though this name stuck to the early, quick picture, it took on an entirely different meaning. For snapshots became almost any picture made casually, even though the subjects were sometimes posed. The history of the snapshot goes back to the early box cameras that were simply pointed at the subject and the shutter release pressed. With the advent of color film, snapshots were made in color as well as black and white. The best description of a snapshot is still a casual, usually unposed, quick picture. All modern cameras are capable of taking snapshots. They are almost exactly the same as what is described as the documentary picture.

The documentary photograph has come to mean a visual record of a moment in history. It usually refers to the pictures made by professional photographers and, more often than not, has been used in connection with the more unpleasant aspects of our civilization. The dust bowl in Oklahoma yielded pictures which showed how farms were swept away, families uprooted and forced to move their few belongings to an area where it would be possible to resettle. There were pictures of migratory workers in California, the sharecroppers of the South, famine in India, war in progress. Documentary pictures, like snapshots, may be either posed or unposed but they are casually made. The photographer is intent upon using a single scene as an example of an historical trend, and approaches the subject with both compassion and professionalism.

Documentary photographs go back to within ten years of the beginning of photography. The first action documentary pictures were made between 1855 and 1860 when Roger Fenton photographed the Crimean War in Balaklava. James Robertson, in 1857, worked with Felice Beato to show the Bengal Sepoy Mutiny in India. By 1861, as war broke out between the North and South in the U.S., Mathew Brady organized his own group of photographers to work out of wagons in which film could be processed. Brady had hired at least nine other photographers. One of them, Alexander Gardner, broke away and formed his own group giving each man credit for his own photographs. The credit line received great impetus when Gardner credited negatives and prints to Timothy O'Sullivan and others who accompanied him to the battlefield.

By now the documentary photograph was well established. The photo-history of world events and social changes has accelerated constantly ever since. Among the best known documentarians between the 1930's and the 1950's were Paul Strand, Walker Evans, Dorothea Lange, Arthur Rothstein, Carl Mydans, Russell Lee and Gordon Parks. Much of the documentation would not have been possible for these people to produce without the development of the so-called candid camera.

The candid photograph. There has been much written about the "candid" photograph. It is a comparatively new form because in the early days of photography films were simply too slow to catch a fleeting gesture, an unposed reflex. When cameras were large and unwieldly there was simply no way to keep the subject from knowing that he was being photographed. It was not until 1928 that Dr. Erich Salomon of Berlin began to use a small, German-built camera, the Ermanox, with an f/2 lens that admitted more light than previous cameras. With this camera and improvements that were made within the next few years, it became possible to make brief exposures without using flash powder or flashbulbs and to obtain unposed, revealing photographs, which soon became known in England and the U.S. as "candid" photographs.

The first of the true candid precision cameras to be marketed in any quantity was the Leica. There had been attempts to make a small effective camera in the U.S. before World War I, but they were not successful. The Leica was dramatically successful and soon pictures of statesmen yawning, scratching their heads or glaring at one another began to appear from time to time in magazines and newspapers throughout the world. The "candid" picture became the trademark of many of the most important photographers of the past generation. Among the pioneers were the German photographer Dr. Paul Wolff and three French photographers: André Kertész, Brassaï, and Henri Cartier-Bresson. Thomas McAvoy, Alfred Eisenstaedt, Peter Stackpole, Robert Capa and many others contributed to the "candid" visual history of the thirties, forties and fifties. From the early thirties natural light photography became a most important photographic technique.

It was not long before the candid camera was adopted by photojournalists. They realized that the small camera, which could be carried anywhere, combined with faster film, would make it possible to show scenes as they happened with greater accuracy and impact on the viewer. With these cameras, pictures were often taken without the knowledge of the subjects. Even if the subjects did know the photographer was present, the camera was so small and inconspicuous that the subjects behaved naturally.

This is one of the differences between the "candid" photograph and the snapshot. The subject is almost always conscious of the camera and in many cases has to hold still for the snapshot to be taken; whereas, with the "candid" photograph, the photographer becomes relatively invisible. Yet, in some ways, as one can easily see from examples shown on these pages, the snapshot, the historical documentary picture and the "candid" photograph have much in common.

The posed picture. This includes portraits (which may range from head shots to bust shots to full figures), family groups and nudes (which do not have to be posed but almost always work out best if they are). (A complete chapter on nude photography will follow.) A pose is technically a position of the head or body. It can be further defined as putting the model into a meaningful attitude that would project an idea which the photographer believes will make an interesting picture.

Posing does not mean stiffness or inflexibility. The model can strike a balanced pose, an easy pose, even a ridiculous or funny pose. It should not imply stiffness, which was the meaning back in the days when it was necessary to put the model's head in a vise to keep it from moving during the long exposure. The pose now is usually photographed almost instantaneously; the model can move from one position to another, the face can change expressions; a profile, a three-quarter view can all be done within the posed picture.

The available or natural light photograph. These are taken with existing light; that is, no light is added in the form of flash or floodlights. With the films and lenses that are now available, it is almost always possible to take pictures with available light indoors or out, day or night. Available light is used by professional photographers in making their candid photographs.

It is ideal for portraits, nudes and both posed and unposed photographs, especially indoors.

The flash picture.   Whether using the electronic flash or flashbulbs, party pictures and informal portraits can be made with inexpensive cameras and with Polaroid cameras. Because a standard distance can be used when flashing the light, exposures can be easily controlled. Almost all modern cameras are equipped for flash use. Electronic flash equipment can be recharged and flashed over and over. Flashbulbs can only be used once. For details see chapter entitled "ARTIFICIAL LIGHT."

Still life.   Photographs of objects can be made with available light, floodlights or flash. Fruits, vegetables, furniture, statuary—all make interesting still life subjects.

Nature.   Although nature pictures can be taken with the pocket type cameras and the Polaroid, they are more effective with the SLR or the viewfinder type cameras. To make effective landscape or seascape pictures, the 35mm negative produces better enlargements than the smaller negative sizes. Interchangeable lenses available for the single lens reflex (SLR) cameras make them more efficient than other types; for example, they can accommodate a telephoto lens, which is important when photographing birds, animals and sometimes distant vistas.

The action photograph.   Action photography, although part of most of the other types of photography, has special qualities. A runner can be stopped dead or slightly blurred or very blurred. In each case, the idea of motion is visualized. A baseball can be stopped in motion just as it touches the player's bat, or a young colt can be shown galloping across a green field. Motion, like light, has many rules. One can photograph in slow motion, medium motion or at high speed. A race driver's car can be stopped while the landscape seems to rush by. A basketball player can be caught in midair with his fingers touching the ball. A prizefighter can be shown midway as he sinks to the canvas floor. Action can even exist in making portraits and snapshots and in candid pictures generally.

Action photographs require choice of the *exact moment.* Unless the photographer selects the most effective moment in the action, he is likely to have an unsatisfactory photograph. A statesman raises his arm in a salute—that is the *exact moment.* A child falls and her subsequent tears illustrate her feelings—that is the *exact moment.* But one man's *exact moment* may not be another's. And here again, as in so many instances in photography, lies the opportunity for expression, for adding your own creative feeling to the picture.

Now that you know what photography is all about, you are ready to take the big step—"SELECTING YOUR CAMERA."

2
SELECTING
YOUR
CAMERA

A camera should be selected in the same way one would select an automobile or a high fidelity sound system, a girl friend or a wife. It should fit your personality; it should be selected in such a way that continuing relations will become more pleasant and more intimate. Unless the beginning photographer can feel completely at ease with the camera, unless it becomes a part of his creative life—then he has selected the wrong camera.

But how to select the right one? This depends upon the use to which you will want to put the camera. Are you going to take a few pictures every month? Do you want to do scenic photographs, close-ups of flowers or telephoto shots of wild life? Do you want to photograph nudes of models or your friends or wife or husband? Do you want to travel with your camera? Are you interested in taking pictures when your subjects are unaware of the camera? Are you completely non-mechanically minded or are you fascinated by gadgetry? These are some of the basic considerations in selecting a camera, plus the all-important one of how much you want to spend. The most expensive one, however, is not necessarily the camera you will feel most at home with, nor is it always the one that will produce the best pictures. For good photographs are not made by the camera. They are created by the person operating it.

Cameras range from the sub-miniature, a pocket type camera that uses a special 9.5mm film, to the giant 11x14 studio camera used by a limited number of professionals to make advertising photographs of food and other still life. In between there are many sizes: the 8x10 studio camera used commercially; the 4 x 5 camera, also widely used commercially and especially by architectural photographers; the 2¼ x 2¼ double lens reflex; the 2¼ x 2¼ single lens reflex. But the great majority of cameras in use today by amateurs and semi-professionals are the 35mm single lens reflex (SLR); the 35mm rangefinder-viewfinder camera; the instant picture cameras exemplified by the Polaroid; and the pocket type cameras best illustrated by Eastman's extensive line of Instamatics.

In the section that follows on cameras you will be able to evaluate each of them according to size, weight, adaptability to various picture taking conditions, ease of loading and handling and price. After reading the "CAMERA" section, and before making your selection, go to your nearest camera store and ask for a tryout. Look through the viewfinder; see whether you can get the picture into focus easily. Have the clerk show you how the camera is loaded and unloaded. If you can, buy a roll of film and run it through the camera using either an exposure meter or, if the exposure is battery controlled, shooting the pictures according to instructions. Give the camera back to the clerk (all this need only take 10 minutes), take your film to be processed (the clerk can probably handle that for you too), then view the film before buying the camera. This is not an essential procedure because all five types of cameras discussed in this book are fully guaranteed, but this is one way of getting the feel of the camera—and why not?

THE CAMERAS

Five types of cameras make up most of the cameras in general use. All of them will produce good pictures in color or black and white. Some are easy to use, some a bit more complex, but none of them require a course in photography. Let's look at them close up and in detail:

The 35mm SLR (Single Lens Reflex). For all-around convenience, size, multiplicity of uses and ease of operation, the 35mm SLR offers more advantages for more different kinds of photographs than any other. This is because lenses are interchangeable, which means that you can take close-ups, portraits, architecture—indeed, almost any subject. It yields color transparencies of the standard 35mm size which fit into all standard projectors, and inexpensive color prints in small and medium sizes are available. In addition, the 35mm film size is big enough, when properly processed, to make excellent black and white enlargements.

Most professional photographers use the 35mm SLR camera. In addition to interchangeable lenses that range from extreme wide angle (meaning you can get a great deal into your picture) to telephoto lenses that allow you to select a detail, cameras of this type also offer what is known as the zoom lens. Having such a lens on your camera supplies you with everything from medium wide angle to normal to telephoto in one lens. It gives the photographer the option of being able to frame the picture exactly as he wants it. The disadvantages of the zoom lens, as opposed to interchangeable lenses in various focal lengths, are that the former is heavier, more expensive and, for some people, more difficult to focus.

But for the beginner who wants to get the feel of different lenses (without purchasing a variety of lenses), the zoom lens is highly recommended. This means you need only the one lens on your camera and do not have to carry three or four others with you. However, when you get to advanced photography, you may find that a wide angle, a normal and a telephoto lens work best for you.

The second most important advantage that the 35mm SLR camera offers is that you actually see the picture right side up directly through the lens—you photograph exactly what you see.

The price range for the 35mm SLR is considerable. The more carefully built the camera, the more automated features it has, the greater the quality and speed range of the shutter (which allows you to take long, slow exposures in dim light or have fast exposures, up to $1/2000$ of a second, in very bright light), the more expensive it is likely to be. In cameras, as in everything else, you get what you pay for, and the highest quality camera with the greatest number of features usually commands the highest price.

But you may not need the extra quality that the highest priced 35mm SLR offers. Technically, you do not need automation at all. It is relatively simple to learn how to read an exposure meter, set the dials at the reading, set the camera controls and take the picture. True, it's not as convenient, it takes longer, and some people simply cannot get the knack of reading exposure meters and converting the information to the camera controls. For them, the fully automated camera is certainly indicated. For anyone it is easier to use—and the automatic features can be switched to manual control.

Because of the various types of films that are available in both color and black and white for the 35mm camera, the different kinds of pictures that can be made with it are infinite. Its size and ease of operation make it an excellent travel camera, candid camera, sports camera and, with certain lenses and specialized films, it can become a scientific instrument capable of microscopic and medical photography. It is the most versatile photographic machine now available.

The 35mm Rangefinder-Viewfinder Camera.   The rangefinder type camera is usually less expensive than the SLR type. While excellent pictures can be taken (it was the pioneer miniature camera) it has two drawbacks:

A. These cameras do not allow you to see directly through the lens but through a window on the upper left-hand corner of the camera. They have a tendency to distort the image and, more important, because of what is known as parallax (a slight difference in view between what the lens sees and what your eye sees), can cause the cropping off of some part of the picture in the final film. It is actually a minor problem and a good viewfinder camera at a low price is adequate for beginning photography.

B. Focusing is done through a rangefinder. Upon looking through the rangefinder two images are seen. The lens barrel of the camera is turned until the two images coincide and the picture is then in focus. But, after focusing, it is usually necessary to move the eye over to the viewfinder to see exactly what you are taking.

The rangefinder type camera usually falls into the medium price range. Some of the outstanding ones feature rangefinder-viewfinder window combined, computerized automatic exposure control and built-in flash connection. So, if you plan to stay in this price range, check out some of the new models.

The Pocket Type Cameras. These include the Instamatic Kodak and other pocket-size cameras. They range from the least expensive non-automated model, which still has most of the advantages of an easy-to-operate camera, to the most expensive model, which is fully automated to take care of most problems of exposure. Lenses range from the slowest f/11 to the fast f/2.7; with either you can take pictures indoors or in dim light by using "fast" film, tripod and cable release.

Almost all of these cameras use cartridge loaded film which is easy to load and unload. It is only necessary to open the camera, slip in the film cartridge, close the camera, push the film advance a couple of times until the number 1 appears, and you're ready to take pictures. Most pocket-size cameras produce 20 pictures with one film loading.

The great majority of these, in the inexpensive range, are fixed-focus cameras, which means you do not have to focus the lens but simply point and shoot. They have only one, or occasionally two, shutter speeds; but some have lenses that focus as close as two feet for close-ups. At least one model has a built-in normal and telephoto lens. The more expensive types also include automatic exposure with a battery-powered electric eye. Flashbulbs or cubes can be used with most models.

These cameras are lightweight, easy to carry, inexpensive and produce reasonably good transparency slides and small color prints. Miniature projectors, including a small circular projector, are manufactured to accommodate the showing of these miniature slides. Many are point-and-shoot cameras where the photographer has little control but must depend upon the brightness of the light and his distance from the subject, because most of these cameras cannot be used at distances closer than five feet.

They make good gifts for the child photographer.

Instant Picture Cameras. This special field of photography is devoted to cameras and film where the final print is developed inside the camera. A range of such cameras are now produced by Polaroid and Eastman Kodak. Both organizations manufacture inexpensive, point and shoot models as well as expensive focusing, electric eye, automatic exposure types.

The cameras are simply designed to produce satisfactory small color prints. If the user is careful, follows the instructions in detail, fair to excellent pictures can be taken. One advantage is that you can see your errors. Should your print not be dark enough, you can adjust the amount of light and take another. If you have moved the camera or don't like the background, you have a second or third try.

Because of construction to accommodate film packs and developing inside the camera, they are comparatively large and somewhat awkward to use. Yet they do the job of delivering the picture on the spot and they are easy to operate. Most of these cameras, even the inexpensive ones, have a built-in electric eye shutter. But this does not mean that you can take pictures in any kind of light. Of course, the lenses are superior on the more expensive models. Inexpensive models often have a red light signal that appears when you begin to push down the release shutter. If this red light flashes, it means there is not enough light to take the picture which keeps you from wasting film.

And film is an important item with all of the instant picture cameras. It is relatively expensive. One must also be careful to see that the rollers inside the camera are kept clean; otherwise, the mechanism may jam or your picture may have uneven development. Again, one must be careful in pulling the picture tab in sequence as each picture is taken for it is possible to jam the camera by pulling the wrong one. This is eliminated in some of the more sophisticated and expensive models where the film changes automatically and the picture is ejected mechanically from the camera.

Most of the above problems are eliminated in the expensive models, but the photographer's finger or fingers must be kept away from the slot through which the picture is ejected. If you want to see what you have taken immediately, there is no substitute for the instant picture cameras. The finished picture comes up, in the case of black and white, within seconds and, in color, within minutes.

There are at least three kinds of situations in which these cameras are superior to all others. It is perfect for parties for everyone can enjoy seeing their picture within minutes after it is taken—and they can take it with them. It is an excellent no risk camera. You can see your mistake immediately and correct it in the next picture. It is a good "making friends" camera. I have used instant cameras quite successfully to develop friendly relations with models and even with primitive people who have rarely, if ever, been photographed before. Some of these people in remote islands and in primitive parts of Africa have believed that their image or spirit could be captured and taken away by the photographer. By taking the image out of the camera and giving it to them, an entirely new relationship can be established.

The use of flash cubes or flash bulbs is recommended. Because the intensity of the flash remains relatively the same for each picture, exposures are likely to be more accurate with flash than daylight. The color of the light varies in daylight from warm to cold and pictures will have, depending upon the time of day, an overall color ranging from blue to orange. With flash, these variations are largely eliminated. There are exceptions. If your subject is surrounded by green walls, the flesh tone is going to have a greenish tinge. You are better off with warm toned or black and white walls for warm toned pictures are generally more pleasing than those with cold tones.

No camera offers as much personal picture privacy. Nudes and semi-nudes of wives, husbands, friends or models are for your eyes alone. No curious local photo finisher ever sees your work. It is the perfect erotic camera. The privacy afforded makes it easier for amateur models to relax and pose for highly personal pictures. You will share the excitement of the picture with your model. There are limitations. For enlargements or duplicates, you must either rephotograph the pictures or send the prints out for duplication.

For professional use, special film holding backs have been developed for both the 2¼ by 2¼ and the 4 by 5 camera. Using these backs, many professional photographers do test shots which show them exactly what they are going to get on either their negative or transparency film. Exposure, details of color and composition can all be checked out. For anyone specializing in portraits, these special backs and instant film not only serve the purpose of testing but help to establish an easy relationship between photographer and subject.

The 2¼ x 2¼ Single Lens Reflex or Twin Lens Camera. Hundreds of professional photographers and thousands of amateurs prefer the 2¼ x 2¼ camera. Its advantages include a larger negative, which means smaller grain and better definition. Changeable lenses make it a versatile instrument in commercial illustration, portraiture and scenic photography. With medium to extreme wide angle lenses it is successfully employed in architectural (especially interior) photography. Interchangeable film cassettes make it possible to change from one film to another in the middle of a shooting sequence. Motors and eye-level sports finders are available.

One of the drawbacks is weight, about twice that of the 35mm single lens reflex, and another is fewer pictures on a roll (12 instead of 20 or 36). These bigger cameras are not as efficient for candid or sports photography and the square format may make composition more complex. Nevertheless, for those advantages listed above, the 2¼ x 2¼ camera, either single or double lens, is highly recommended.

3
LIGHT, NATURE AND NATURAL LIGHT

The Biblical admonition "Let there be light" accurately describes the most important single element in photography. Pictures, although recorded on film, are created entirely by light—not only sunlight, the soft, misty light of dawn or twilight, but also man-made light. The two forms of light in photographic terms are called natural light and artificial light and every picture is taken with either one or the other or a combination of both. Every light condition can be photographed with modern film and modern cameras. Anything that can be seen with the eye can be photographed and the picture taken in such a way that it will show the same variations in light intensity as the scene itself.

It is even possible to take pictures in the dark, using infrared light and film that is sensitive to the infrared radiations. This, however, is a very special field used to aid medical diagnoses and in the evaluation of certain minerals. It has been used successfully to capture the habits of nocturnal animals whose movements cannot be seen with the eye. It is also used in aerial reconnaisance and mapping, for infrared film, properly filtered, cuts through atmospheric haze very effectively.

Light comes in all colors and the photographer should become used to seeing not only the intensity of light but its color as well. Early morning light before sunrise has a blue tinge because the sun has not added visible yellow. Pictures taken at dawn have the appearance of dawn; that is, flesh tones will have a bluish cast, landscapes a gray-blue appearance. Then the early morning sun effects a transformation and even shaded areas become less blue. Pictures taken in the early morning while the sun is on a long slant will often seem to be too yellow. But that's the way the light is. The early morning sun does contain more yellow than it does later in the day.

For the last 50 years photographers have suffered from very poor advice from film manufacturers who recommended that pictures be made in sunlight after 10 in the morning and before 4 in the afternoon. This was originally true because films were far slower than they are now and lenses admitted much less light. However, pictures taken during these hours (except those backlighted or in shade) are harsh, flat and generally lack tonal values. Midday is the worst possible time to make outdoor portraits in the sun. The subject stands squinting from the sun, eyes almost closed. Heavy shadows form below the eye sockets, the nose, the lips and the chin, and there is almost no way to correct this. All children dread the ordeal of taking pictures in the sun because it hurts their eyes and not even threats or promises can get a smile out of them. So from 10 A.M. to 4 P.M. avoid the sun or use it in back of the subject and carefully shade the camera lens from the direct sunlight. Better still, move your subject into the shade, but be careful if you are using color film for light reflects colors and if there is green grass in the foreground and green trees on each side, there is likely to be a greenish cast to the flesh tones. This can be avoided by moving the model away from the reflected sidelight. Many of the best soft natural light portraits can be done in open shade or on an overcast day when there is no sun and therefore no heavy shadows.

The problems of color reflection, of course, do not exist when the photographer is doing portraits in black and white. It then does not matter whether there is a green reflection coming from the trees for it will have no visual effect on the black and white film. So stay out of the harsh direct sunlight. Remember, too, it is often helpful to use the sun for backlighting to bring out the highlights on the subject's hair while using a large sheet of white cardboard or an inexpensive umbrella-type reflector to throw a soft light onto the subject's face.

Landscapes, like people's features, flatten out when the sun is high overhead. As with portraits, the worst time of day to take landscapes is roughly between 10 A.M. and 4 P.M. The best landscape pictures are those which capture a mood on film which, when projected as slides or large prints made from negatives, evoke memories of the time and place that the photographs were taken. All modern cameras and films are capable of recording sunsets, scenes at dawn, or vistas when long shadows lie across the plains or mountains. Sometimes, when the light is very dim indeed, the exposure may be a long one and this means that the camera should be wedged or braced against the window of your car, a tree or on a light-weight tripod. With most 35mm single lens reflex cameras, and many of the new pocket types, a tripod will be unnecessary, but a car door, window, fender, fence post, highway sign, etc., may serve very well if your exposure is longer than a 50th of a second, for even at that speed it is worth trying to find a solid base to avoid camera motion.

Paying attention to all of the above advice about light will generally give you softer, better modeling in your portraits and more dramatic landscapes. But there are times when you'll want to take pictures between the hours of 10 A.M. and 4 P.M. and when the subject you want to photograph is in the direct sun. Pictures of sporting events can be very effectively photographed in full sunlight. For one thing, it's possible to use a high shutter speed of 1/500 to 1/1000 to stop the motion and in bright light there will still be considerable depth to the picture as well. You can always find a shaded location when you are making a portrait but a series of candid pictures taken at a picnic can be effective in full sunlight, as can those taken of people at the beach and even mountain climbing. While rules are important for portraits and landscapes generally, almost all photographic rules can be broken to get the spontaneity of a snapshot of children or adults at play.

Knowledge of light can add tremendously to the effectiveness of every photograph you make. Let's take travel, for instance. You arrive at your destination in the early afternoon and, of course, you want to take pictures right away. Don't do it. Wait until at least an hour before sundown. Then look around and see how the light looks and whether there is a scene worth adding to your collection. It may be that the light at 6 o'clock in the evening will make for a much more interesting picture, possibly an even more interesting one when you first awake in the morning. Try to train your eye to see into shadows and note how much softer colors become.

If you have trained your eye to see the different colors and different intensities of light, then, when you look through the viewfinder of the camera at the scene you are planning to photograph, you will be able to see the brightness, the shadows and the color combinations, and be ready to move the camera to compose those elements in the most pleasing way before pushing the shutter release.

Your camera can reintroduce you to nature. Scenes dimly remembered from childhood, early imprints on your senses from camp and camping trips can be rediscovered with a camera as your companion. For a camera, after you have become familiar with its use, becomes like a friend on a walk through the woods or a stroll through a garden. It is a surprisingly personal being with whom you can share your vision silently and without fear of criticism or comment.

Nature offers an incredible variety of subjects. Broad vistas open up as you stand at a viewpoint and watch the movement of shadows across the landscape caused by clouds moving across the sky. Watching the subtle changes in light gives you an opportunity to evaluate the scene and to compose a pleasing landscape picture. It is important not to take a landscape the instant you see it. Learn to let the eye explore first what the camera will record. Remember that present-day film is highly sensitive and that scenes in the very late afternoon light, even after sundown, can be photographed. The light of early morning has similar characteristics to that of late afternoon. Long shadows give depth and shape to the scene, and the golden light of dawn and sunset are extremely effective when you're using color film.

Walking with a camera will teach you a great deal about its operation for you will be faced with wooded areas where little light penetrates, with brilliantly lit landscapes, with the movement of rivers, streams, brooks and waterfalls. One of the great advantages of the manually-operated camera—one that allows the photographer to decide how fast the shutter moves and how large the lens opening is—can be seen when photographing a moving stream. For a very slow shutter, perhaps an exposure of a 25th of a second, or even less, if the camera is on a light tripod or propped against a tree, shows the water moving more effectively than the fast shutter speed that freezes the motion. Again, you may wish to have the background sharp and clear with a feeling of restless leaves in the foreground. A slow speed will give the windblown feeling to the leaves while the background remains crisp and sharp.

But first learn to use the automatic features if the camera has them. This can give a perfect exposure of a bee on a blossom, a butterfly in flight, or a lizard poised precariously on a plant. You need not venture very far from your home or your car to explore wild places as well as well-traveled paths. The late famous photographer Edward Steichen spent years photographing a single tree in all of its seasonal variations. Nature offers every kind of model. Somewhere not too far away there is a bird's nest, a flower just bursting into bloom; the dogwood is decorating the countryside or the vividly colored autumn leaves are beginning to fall. All of these make excellent subjects and become a permanent record of the way nature looks to you.

Because shutters on modern cameras move at a rapid speed, and because both black and white and color film have extraordinary sensitivity, you can record the flight of a single bird or an abstract pattern of ducks flying against the dark sky. So carry a camera in your car or on your walks and before you set out make a simple decision: Am I going to photograph in black and white or in color? If your camera has interchangeable lenses, take along a telephoto type or a zoom lens. Best of the zoom lenses for nature is the 45 to 90mm, which gives you a medium telephoto and a fairly wide angle as well. Another is the macro type, which allows you to make dramatic close-ups 2 or 3 inches away from the subject. But neither of these lenses are absolutely essential. You can take excellent pictures with the inexpensive pocket types and have enlargements made of the section you want to display, and many of these have a close-up attachment. The Polaroid SX-70 has a special front element allowing close-ups of objects as near as 12 inches from the camera. This makes it useful for flower photography. More on lenses in Chapter 4.

There is no limit to the fascinating forms and textures in nature. Remember that you are not trying to reproduce nature as you see it, but rather to see nature with a fresh view and then make a permanent record of that view. So give your eyes time to see and reflect upon the pictures. Then transfer the information from your eyes to the eye of the camera.

Flying on commercial airlines offers opportunities for interesting pictures—and even more uninteresting ones. Best subjects are cities (just after take-off and before landing), canyons, lakes, rivers and mountains. Make your seat reservation

early and always in front *of the wing—otherwise the jet airstream will ruin the pictures. These pictures of Mount Hood were shot moments apart, using a zoom lens at 43mm for the long shot, 86mm for the medium closeup. Infrared film, 25A filter.*

The deeply etched rocks showed lines like those of a very old person's face. To bring them out I waited until the light was at a 90-degree angle from my camera and used a polarizing filter to darken both the water and the sky.

A simple but effective and almost abstract picture of black and gray pebbles in the surf at Big Sur, California, a great scenic area. An inexpensive pocket camera was used from the bank above, with my hand shading the lens from the sun.

Depth and perspective are the essential elements in this documentary photo-graph of the good earth. The SLR camera was focused on the twig, right center. The lens setting was f/22 and the exposure, with medium fast film, 1/125.

On the island of Dominica lies another world—the land of the Carib Indians. I wanted to suggest the narrow pathway—the almost impenetrable jungle beyond. Needing depth, I waited for bright sunlight, photographed at f/22.

Deeply impressed upon almost all amateur and some professional photographers is the rule that sunlight is the best time for taking pictures and that rainy, stormy and cloudy days are to be avoided. It takes a long time to realize that this is

*untrue. Interesting light, no matter what the weather, makes interesting pic-
tures. This sudden rainstorm on an Iowa prairie was taken from my automobile.
I focused at infinity and let the electronic shutter of the automatic SLR take over.*

As I was driving along a Canadian byway, the natural beauty of a backlighted forest stopped me. There was no breeze, yet the shimmering sunlight filtering through the trees gave the effect of motion to this photograph of a birch grove.

While retracing the footsteps of Abraham Lincoln, I walked along the trail to his birthplace near Hodgenville, Kentucky. To recreate the atmosphere of his time, I placed an ax (said to have belonged to him) in silhouette against a tree.

I found this odd tree (or perhaps it found me, I've never been quite sure but it seemed to be waving) in the Joshua Tree National Monument in southeastern California. Automatic exposure, no filter, pocket-size camera.

There were many ways to see this misshapen dying Joshua tree. I saw it as a giant insect from outer space. How you photograph shapes depends entirely on your point of view... or how you respond to the Rorschach test.

A deep gorge in the Rocky Mountains with a waterfall in the far background was photographed with a normal lens on a rangefinder 35mm camera. The day was overcast, which helped to add detail to shadow areas. Fine grain film.

Cypress trees covered with moss grow in the swamps of the Louisiana bayou country. Enough early morning light had filtered through the trees to allow an exposure at 1/125 of a second from the canoe that I was paddling.

Niagara Falls may be the most photographed site in the world, yet seen from your own viewpoint it can yield fresh dramatic pictures. This one, taken from a sightseeing boat in the early morning, has effective crosslighting.

Infrared film with a 25A red filter and a 200mm telephoto lens were used to take this original mountain landscape. The location was the United States portion of Glacier National Park in northwestern Montana near Canadian border.

4
EXPOSURE, LENSES, SHUTTERS AND FOCUSING

If the picture is too dark, it is underexposed—*not enough light* has reached the sensitive film. If the picture is too light, it is overexposed—*too much light* has been allowed to reach the film. When taking a black and white photograph, if too much light enters through the lens and shutter the negative film will be heavy and dark. This means that, when it is printed as a positive, it will be too light and overexposed. Again, if not enough light strikes the film, the negative will be light or thin and the resulting picture will be dark, or underexposed.

Negative color film from which prints are made directly operate exactly the same way with regard to exposure as black and white film. For all practical purposes, the same is true for color transparencies, since these are negative films that are reversed into positives during processing. So the most important thing to know about exposure is: Enough light (not too little—not too much) must be transmitted through the lens and shutter to the film.

But how to be sure of this "perfect" exposure, to create a picture that is neither too light nor too dark?

If you are using a manually operated camera without a built-in exposure device: Set the camera controls for shutter speed and lens (f stop) opening at the film speed and aperture called for in the instructions that come with each roll of film. For example, let's assume you are using black and white film with a speed rating of ASA (American Standards Association) 400. (What does this 400 mean? It means that the film is more sensitive to light than a film rated ASA 160. ASA ratings start at 0.8 for the least sensitive film and go up to ASA 25,000 for the most sensitive film made so far.) Your instruction sheet will show that you may take photographs in bright sunlight at 1/500 of a second at f/16. You may wish to stop the motion of a surfer riding the waves at the beach, a runner on the sand, or a skier as he speeds down a run. You may photograph any of these at the indicated exposure, but you will freeze the motion more effectively if you open the diaphragm one f stop to f/11 and double the shutter speed to 1/1000. The same amount of light will enter the camera but, because the lens opening is longer, the shutter speed can be shorter. You will not always be at the beach or in the snow. For average sunlit scenes your instructions will show 1/250 at f/16 and will advise you to open up the lens—from f/22 to f/11—for close-ups where the light is behind the subject. But suppose the weather changes. Under a heavily overcast sky or in a well-shaded area the lens opening becomes f/8 at the same 1/250 of a second.

Once you understand that the shutter speeds and lens openings are related, you may choose any number of combinations. One one-thousandth of a second at f/11 admits exactly the same amount of light as 1/500 at f/16 or 1/250 at f/22. As the lens opening is decreased you get more depth in the picture but the shutter speed becomes slower. This relationship of lens to shutter continues through all camera speeds. For instance, suppose you have two lamps in your bedroom at night. You can still photograph with fast black and white film, but the lens must be fully open and the camera must be held steady because of the relatively slow shutter speed of 1/30 of a second. A good way to visualize the process is to picture a garden hose with the water turned on. If the nozzle is made smaller (called "stopped down" in photography) the stream of water shoots out for a greater distance in a smaller stream. This is the depth effect you get when you stop down the lens. As the lens is opened up, the beam of light becomes less sharp. You do not get as much depth in the picture.

It is of absolute importance that you know the ASA speed of the film, for not even the most automatic camera can tell what film you are going to put into it. But almost all cameras have a dial that can be set at the ASA speed of the film. Once this is done your fully automated camera can, because of a battery-operated electronic cell, automatically open and close the diaphragm or increase or decrease the shutter speed to make a reasonably accurate exposure. Think of the ASA speed simply as a number. The higher the number the more sensitive the film. When you look at the printed instructions with each roll of film remember that you do not have to follow it slavishly. So long as you know one exposure that includes the right combination of lens opening and shutter speed, you can select a speed and opening consistent with the requirements of your picture. To get great depth (everything in focus from foreground to background) on an overcast day, you can shoot your picture at f/22 at 1/30 of a second; or, if the subject is moving and you need no depth, at f/4 at 1/1000.

There is far more latitude for exposure with black and white film than with color, because after processing it is possible to use printing paper with more or less contrast to correct overexposure or underexposure to some degree. But a good average exposure will always yield good prints. Underexposed or overexposed film can yield fairly good prints, depending upon the degree of variation from the norm.

Negative color film allows for minor corrections but, because color printing paper does not have nearly so much latitude as black and white printing paper, exposures must be close to normal. With color transparencies there is no chance to correct after exposure, because the type of color film that is used to make transparencies when processed becomes a transparency which may be too light or too dark. There is no way to correct this.

There is a story about a distinguished Japanese photographer who spoke before one of the large camera clubs. At the end of the meeting he was asked how he determined with such extreme accuracy the various exposures for both his high-key and low-key photographs. He hesitated for just a moment and then said:

"When I first started photography, I bought my camera and a roll of film. When I opened the film, inside the cardboard box was a little piece of paper. It told me what to do to expose this film properly—and I have been doing it ever since."

I highly recommend using the film instructions and using your camera manually until you are used to it, even if it is an automatic type. After you know what the camera will do manually, then switch to automatic and, if you continue to get good pictures, stick with it. But be sure to keep a fresh battery handy for, when your battery goes, so does your automatic exposure mechanism. Then, unless you know what to do with manual operation, you won't be able to continue to take pictures. There is a battery-check button on most automatics—check it often.

What about exposure meters? There are plenty of good ones and an hour's concentration, at most, should be enough for anyone to learn about their operation. Basically, there are two types of meters:

1. The first is pointed at the subject, a release button is pushed and a needle operated by a photoelectric cell indicates a number. This number is matched to a pointer on the dial and then the correct exposure can be read on a supplementary dial. It is necessary, however, as with your camera, first to set the speed of the film you are using in the appropriate place on the exposure meter, because unless the meter knows what kind of film you are using it cannot come up with the right exposure.

It is especially important with the reflector type meter that it not be pointed upward at the sky and it is usually best that it be tilted slightly downward because the sky is usually much brighter than any other part of the picture. What you want is the average light reading for the scene.

2. Some meters combine both the reflector principle and an incident light reading attachment. To read incident light, hold the meter in the position of the subject and point it at the camera. This allows the light that will fall upon the subject to be read. It is as if the camera were photographing the light falling upon the meter rather than the light reflected from the subject.

Let's take a step-by-step approach to determine exposure. The subject is a person standing in an open shaded area. You are going to take a portrait. According to the written instructions with the color film, your speed is ASA 64. This means the exposure will be approximately 1/125 of a second at f/4. Now, let's check that with your reflector type meter. Set the meter for ASA 64, point it at the subject's face from a distance of about 18 inches, press the release button, match up the number that is exposed to the pointer on the meter, and you should be able to read on the exposure dial that your exposure is 1/125 at f/4. Or, if you wish, 1/250 at f/2.8, 1/500 at f/2, 1/1000 at f/1.4. If you feel a bit shaky, the 1/250 at f/2.8 might be your best bet for that would give you enough depth—that is, the background would be soft and out of focus—yet there would be little likelihood of camera motion.

That piece of convex glass that was placed over the pinhole in the darkroom of the ancient *camera obscura* has proliferated into literally hundreds of different kinds of lenses. With them all kinds of magic can be performed: figures elongated, heads distorted, distant people brought up close, close up people pushed farther away, multiple images produced on a single film, an insect's eye; or a completely camouflaged missile bunker photographed in detail from half a mile away. There may not be too many of these effects that you are going to want to create but one never knows—and you should learn enough about lenses to be able to buy the kind that best suits your needs. Here are some of the facts about vision and lenses that will help.

You will find that, as a photographer, you view things through lenses quite otherwise than you would ordinarily. As you begin to take pictures, you will develop a sense of awareness that allows you to view a scene before you in its entirety. Then, certain elements are instantly eliminated as your photographer's eye recomposes the picture. This kind of picture (taking in all that your normal vision sees) is called a long shot. It records the entire scene, but composed as you want it composed. Then the scene becomes fragmented as your photographer's eye focuses sharply on certain elements.

For instance, let's take a group of people dining. You walk into the room, see the entire table with food on it: the diners, all eight of them, seated; a lamp visible in the corner; the serving table nearby. Two candles are on the table and a picture is on the wall in the background. You view this overall scene and move your head to one side or the other, eliminating elements that seem extraneous or unnecessary. Actually, you may take this picture only with your eyes.

Next, you focus on two people in an intimate discussion. Your eyes compose a picture which includes the flickering light of the candle in the foreground, thus helping to establish the mood. The scene can be further fragmented. The picture may be only of a candle with an interesting face of a man or woman in the background, or you may focus on the candelabra with the people out of focus but softly delineated in the background. In this one scene, you may compose and focus on at least five to ten interesting photographs.

All cameras come equipped with some kind of lens. Almost all lenses are made of glass but it is possible to make lenses out of clear plastic or quartz. The function of the lens is to gather the light rays coming from the subject at which it is directed, then to transfer the image to the film plane. The distance from the lens to the film allowing a sharp image from a distant subject to be reflected onto the film is called the focal length of the lens. All lenses have this focal length engraved on their barrels, usually in millimeters—(25.4 millimeters are equal to one inch). The smaller the number of millimeters, the greater the area the lens covers. For example, an SLR camera with an 8mm "fish eye" lens would allow the camera to see a 180 degree view, or approximately what your eyes can see if you look as far as possible to the right and left without moving your head. There are many wide angle lenses between the 8mm "fish eye" and the so-called normal objective lens of 50-55mm. Should you use a wide angle lens for anything except especially distorted effects (which you get with the "fish eye" lens), it is important that you have a lens that does not distort. This means that, on a 35mm camera, your wide angle lens cannot be wider than 18mm or distortion is noticeable. The advantage of wide angle lenses is not only that they take in a greater area than normal or telephoto lenses but that, because of their construction, they can bring the entire scene in focus at a reasonably large aperture, or lens opening.

We have pointed out that as the millimeters increase the amount of area that the lens covers decreases. The 50mm lens gives an approximate view of what you see when your eyes are concentrated on a central spot and are not trying to see to the edges of your vision. From this point on, lenses become relatively telescopic and are called telephoto lenses. However, the 85mm or 90mm lens, which is excellent for portraits, could be put into the category of semi-telephoto. Telephoto lenses range from roughly 85mm to 1000mm. As they bring the object up closer to the film, they become larger and heavier. The 1000mm lens will be very bulky indeed.

Another way to say this is that the shorter the lens, the smaller the individual image will be on the film. As the focal length is increased, the individual image becomes larger. For example, imagine that you are standing 50 feet away from an elephant. With a wide angle lens the elephant will appear quite small, and around him you will see the trees, grass, hills—in fact, so much of the landscape that the elephant is only an incidental part of it. With a normal lens you will see the elephant's body, trunk and a small amount of the scene around him. He has become much bigger on the film. With a medium telephoto lens of 85mm or 105mm you will see only the elephant and none of the foliage or landscape. A 200mm lens will allow you to see about half of the elephant. With a 500mm lens you will see only his head. And with a 1000mm lens you will photograph only the elephant's eye.

You will rarely want to take along all of these lenses. Indeed, the 500mm and 1000mm lenses can be considered as special rather than standard equipment. Over the years I have found that a 20mm wide angle, a 55mm normal, an 85mm semi-telephoto and a 200mm telephoto lens will cover almost every professional photographic need. When I am traveling and cannot get to the various lenses packed away, I carry a zoom lens on the camera. This lens has an adjustable focal length. In one lens it combines all focal lengths between 45mm, which is nearly normal, and 90mm, which is semi-telephoto. Excellent for photographing animals, tame or wild ones, a zoom lens with a range of from 80mm to 200mm is almost an essential. This means that you are starting with a semi-telephoto and going up to a very real telephoto that will bring the subject in quite close. New zoom lenses are being developed continuously and, for the beginning photographer who only plans on one lens, they are a good buy.

Yet the average amateur need not go this far. With your pocket subminiature you can move in close enough to the subject to enlarge the image on the film simply by your proximity to it. The same holds true for other cameras, automatic and non-automatic, or even the self-processing Polaroids. Most cameras allow you to move up to within 3 feet or less of the subject and to move back far enough to take in a landscape.

The selection of a lens has much to do with the kind of pictures you plan to take. There are some lenses adapted for special uses. For instance, a macro lens can be used as a normal lens but with it you can do extreme close-ups. Some macro lenses automatically adjust for the increased exposure that is necessary when the central front element of the lens is extended longer than its focal length indicates. In other words, a macro 50mm lens, when it is extended to do extreme close-up work, becomes more than 50mm and, unless it has an automatic exposure compensation device built into it, the exposure must be increased.

One professional technique for close-up pictures is to purchase a reversal ring for the normal lens on your 35mm SLR camera. The lens is taken off, reversed and put back on the camera. This will allow you to focus some 8 to 10 inches closer and give you an extreme close-up effect. The lens must, however, be set at infinity and instead of focusing with the barrel of the lens, one must move the camera backward or forward until the subject comes into sharp focus. Exposure must be figured from an exposure meter. My experience has been that it is hardly worth the trouble and that an inexpensive supplementary lens to fit over your regular lens is the simplest and most inexpensive way for the amateur to take close-ups. Most of these lenses come in plus 1, plus 2 or plus 3. The higher the number, the closer you can get to your subject. Such supplementary close-up lenses are even available for many of the sub-miniature cameras and for the Polaroid types.

If figures interest you, it is possible to take a picture with a lens that will cover 220 degrees or with a telephoto lens that will magnify the object 40 times. If you are going in for expensive equipment, by all means buy good lenses. They usually cost more than the bargain type but they are invariably worth it. But do not start collecting lenses. They begin to be a drawback instead of an asset to your photography after a certain point. You must depend upon your own vision—move in or out as you see fit with your camera and carry as few lenses as possible with you.

You should care for your lenses the same way you care for your eyes. Scratches will injure them and they should be kept dust free. A drop of lens cleaning solution used from time to time and wiped off carefully with a soft cotton cloth will remove any accumulation of grime. But lenses should be checked and dust accumulation wiped off with every use. This can be done with a face tissue or a soft cloth.

Care should be taken not to drop lenses, for lens mounts can be dented easily and the glass chipped. When not in use, extra lenses should be kept in either a leather lens case or a soft padded pouch. It is best to use lens covers on both ends.

When checking the camera that you intend to buy, be sure to note whether the interchangeable lens mount works smoothly and easily and whether the lens locks gently into position. Of the two types of mounts, bayonet or screw, I prefer the bayonet. But there are many good lenses that come in screw mounts. These can often be adapted to bayonet mounts.

The shutter is a curtain that opens briefly, allowing the light traveling through the lens to reach the film. There are two basic types of shutters. One is called a *leaf* or *between-the-lens* shutter. It opens when its metal leaves fan outward, leaving a hole for the light to pass through. This shutter is confined, generally, to the rangefinder cameras and to the inexpensive pocket types. Because of the mechanical construction of this shutter, the minimum time for which most of them can be opened is 1/250 of a second, which is fast enough to stop some, but by no means all, action. Some shutters are electronically programmed. Others use a spring release mechanism.

The 35mm SLR cameras use a focal plane shutter. This is a metal or cloth curtain that moves across the opening in front of the film, allowing the light to strike the film briefly.

It is possible to set the shutter for a manually timed exposure, which means that the shutter stays open from the time the release is pressed down until it is pressed again to close it. A pause exposure is one where the release is depressed, the shutter opens but closes when the pressure on the release is removed. It is also possible to set the shutter release for a sequence of speeds ranging from one second to 1/1000 of a second. The slower speeds admit more light to the film, the faster speeds less. The slower speeds give more depth to the picture, which means that both foreground and distant objects can be in focus. Fast speeds clip off the light so rapidly that action can be stopped. For most photographs a compromise between the two is best. With color film, it is usually possible to set the shutter at 1/125 or 1/250 of a second, speeds that will eliminate blur from camera motion and still keep foreground and background in focus for average scenes at 12 feet or more.

Shutters are delicate mechanisms and they are rarely absolutely accurate. A reading of 1/125 may be only 1/100 of a second; 1/500 may be only 1/400; 1/1000 is usually about 1/800. If your shutter is slow, you will get too light, or overexposed, pictures every time. It is rare for a shutter to be too fast. There are two ways of testing your shutter speed. First, be sure to set the film speed dial at the ASA setting indicated in the instructions that accompany the film. Then, if you have an automatic camera, shoot the roll of film. If it is a non-automatic camera, use an exposure meter. If the resulting transparencies are too light or if the negatives are too dark, your shutter speeds are slow.

The second way, and certainly the surest, is to take the camera to the nearest repair shop where, for a nominal cost, the shutter speeds can be checked quickly and accurately. You will then be given a card listing the actual speed. This may sound more serious than it really is. A small difference between shutter speeds is not noticeable in the film. But it is good to know that, if most of your transparencies come out on the light side or most of your black and white negatives seem overexposed, the shutter speed is at fault...then you can compensate by stopping down the lens slightly.

If it is important for you to take pictures quietly and inconspicuously, you might listen to the shutter as it is released on a number of cameras. Some shutters go off with a thwack that can be heard for considerable distances. Others are relatively quiet. There are times when a quiet shutter is an absolute essential. Photographers who take publicity and promotion pictures on movie sets or at stage rehearsals are often banned if the shutter noise is disturbing. Even if you are using the available light (which you should be) at an amateur or professional theatrical production, a loud shutter annoys everyone around you. So when you are selecting your camera, keep in mind that you don't want it to be too noisy.

Most photographers try to avoid making double exposures and almost all modern cameras have been engineered so double exposures are just about impossible. But double exposures, if carefully planned, can result in extremely interesting pictures. Many of the 35mm cameras have a release button, usually on the rewind mechanism, which allows the shutter to be reset without advancing the film, thereby making a double exposure possible. Why make a double exposure? Because using a black background, it is possible to take one model, expose the film with electronic flash, move the model a step sideways and flash again, have her move another step sideways and flash a third time. You'll find you have all three images slightly overlapped on the one piece of film. Again, with a black background, the model can be draped in black with only her arms out and bent. Take one exposure, recock the shutter, move the arms upward and flash again, recock the shutter, move the arms down and this time take the black drape off the model and flash. In the resulting picture your model will have six arms and yet she can be accurately exposed. The possibilities for double exposure pictures are infinite, and most professional photographers use this effective technique.

Shutters deteriorate just as people do from lack of exercise. So even if your camera is not in regular use, take it out of the drawer or closet occasionally, wind and release the shutter a few times. But don't leave the shutter cocked when the camera is not in use: having the winding mechanism tensed will not do it any good. And remember, when you're taking pictures, be sure to move the shutter-winding film advance lever all the way over. It is the only way to be sure the shutter is fully wound and will release properly.

ABOUT FILTERS AND FILTER FACTORS

Whether or not you use a filter over your lens will depend upon the final result you want. If your only purpose is to reproduce the scene just as it looks, you won't need a filter. But if you want to make any changes in the light, contrast or values, then the use of a filter becomes imperative.

What is a filter? It is a piece of optically flat colored glass, sometimes even an optically flat clear piece of glass, such as an UV (ultraviolet) filter, sometimes known as a haze filter. These filters do not require a change in exposure. They reduce the amount of ultraviolet light which means that the picture, to some extent, can be clearer as a result of haze reduction. It works equally well with black and white or color. It has an additional purpose: even if it does not cut through all the haze, it does protect your lens from dust and scratches. Like the lens, it should be kept clean.

Second on the professional list would be a polarizing filter. This is used to reduce or eliminate reflections (just as in polarizing eyeglasses), reduce or eliminate glare and cut down on haze. An additional function, and sometimes the most important one, is that it can be used to darken the sky. The polarizing filter works well with either black and white or color film. In color film you will find that the color values are darker, the picture seems not quite real in its richness, colors are more subdued and the overall tone of the picture is darker and less brilliant. Yet it is also more dramatic; skies are deep blue and haze is reduced to a minimum.

42

You must open up your lens approximately one and a half f stops more than normal for the polarizing filter has a factor of approximately two and a half times the normal exposure. Polarizing filters can be used on any camera, but must be rotated until they are at the angle of their greatest efficiency. When using a polarizing filter for through-the-lens viewing you can turn the filter until you see the reflections disappear and the sky darken. Should you be using any camera without through-the-lens viewing, hold the filter up to your eye and turn it until the sky darkens and the reflections disappear, then be sure to place it on the lens at that same angle.

These are the two filters that I recommend for use with color, unless you want to have an overall red, green or yellow scene, for that is exactly what a black and white color filter (that is, a colored filter for black and white film) will do to your color film.

The contrast and the color values that are translated into black and white when you're using panchromatic (black and white) film can be managed, usually for the better, by using the popular K2 filter. This is a medium yellow filter which blocks out much of the blue sky, rendering it a more pleasant, deep gray tone. It is also effective for separating cloud formations rather than having the entire sky go white as it normally would.

With black and white filters it is only necessary to know that if you want anything in the picture to be lighter in color, use the same color filter on the camera. If there is any object that you want to be darker in the picture, use that color filter on the camera. For instance, a bowl of red apples photographed normally will render the apples quite dark. But if we photograph them (remember, this is black and white) with a #25 red filter, the apples will be very light. If we wanted to render a bowl of green apples light colored, we would use a green filter. So the formula is simple: use same color filters for making objects lighter; opposite color filters for making them darker. Some architectural forms are often rendered much more effective by using a red filter which turns the blue sky in the background black, allowing the structure to stand out in dramatic contrast.

All filters, with the exception of the ultraviolet, require additional exposure. Be sure to check the instructions with the filter when you buy it, and carefully note whether it is a 2X (which means twice the exposure), 2½X, or 3X (three times the exposure) type. On a 2X filter twice the normal exposure is required. You will open your lens one f stop or change the shutter to a slower speed (for instance, from 1/250 to 1/125). If you are using the filter on a single lens reflex camera with automatic exposure, or electronic readout exposure, you need not be concerned about the filter factors, for they are taken care of by the electronic system. However, I have found it safer, when using heavy red or green filters—or even polarizing filters—to change over to manual, use an exposure meter and figure the filter factor myself.

You will find filters easier to use if they can be screwed directly onto your lens rather than used in a filter holder. There is another advantage of the screw-in filter. It does not fall off easily and it fits closely to the lens. Some filter holders extend out so far that, when a lens shade is used with them, they may cut into or shadow the edges of your picture.

Two more specialized filters should be mentioned. Electronic flash has a tendency to contain too much light on the blue end of the spectrum. Therefore, an 81A or 81B filter may be necessary to give warm enough flesh tones in your speedlight flash photography.

Perhaps the oldest photographic joke (dating back to the turn of the century) concerns two young women who go to a photographer's studio to have their pictures taken. He poses them and then gets under a large black cloth which completely covers his head and shoulders. One girl anxiously asks the other, "What's he going to do under there?" The other answers, "He's going to focus." The first girl exclaims, incredulously, "Both of us!"

But jokes aside, to make pictures sharp it has always been necessary, except with the small inexpensive fixed-focus lens on some pocket cameras, to move the lens toward or away from the film so that the light rays reflecting the scene fall sharply on the film. As the scene changes from a blur to a well defined picture it comes into focus. To take a close-up, the camera is moved forward, and the lens is moved forward, (that is, away from the film) as well. To take a wider scene, such as a landscape, the lens is moved back to what is called infinity; that is, as far back as it will go. This puts everything into focus beyond a few feet directly in front of the camera. When the smallest lens opening is used, even the immediate foreground becomes sharply defined.

Focusing is vital in the operation of all 35mm cameras and in most of the moderately expensive pocket cameras and Polaroids. Out-of-focus pictures probably make up more than half of the ruined pictures that photographers take. Yet it requires just a little more time and care to be sure the image is completely sharp. In the rangefinder cameras, where there is a split image, the two images converge when the picture is in focus. All single lens reflex cameras have a method of focusing through the lens. The subject is blurred until the lens barrel, or focusing ring, is turned and then the image becomes completely sharp. There is a spot in the center of the picture upon which the photographer can concentrate. When the dots in that spot become sharply defined, the picture is in perfect focus. Some SLR cameras also use a combination of the sharp dot and the two converging images.

My personal preference is the single lens reflex camera, partly because of the problem known as parallax in the rangefinder type camera, which has been mentioned in Chapter 2. It is very easy to slice off the top of a person's head when working close up with a rangefinder or viewfinder type camera. On some of them, the lenses are fixed; there are no interchangeable lenses. However, on the single lens reflex camera, no matter what lens you put on it, you photograph what you see. If it is sharp, it will be sharp in the finished photograph.

If you expect to take pictures on the spur of the moment, as is often the case when traveling, for example, it is a good idea to keep your camera set at the relative focusing range and exposure adequate for a picture that might occur. Let's say you are walking down a street watching the other side and suddenly you see a colorful flower vendor with an equally colorful customer directly across from you. If you have your camera focused at about 25 feet (assuming you have ASA 64 film in the camera and it is a reasonably bright day) and your exposure has been set for 1/125 of a second at f/8, all you have to do is lift the camera to eye level, get the scene in your viewfinder and press the shutter. Because of your prefocusing and presetting of the exposure, you get the picture.

If you have an automatic camera, you will still have to focus but you won't have to worry about the exposure. The internal exposure meter will take care of that. It's a good idea to practice this technique of prefocusing and it's especially valuable at sports events or when photographing moving objects.

While we are on the subject of focusing, let's also discuss depth of field, or the area in sharp focus in front of and behind the focal point. For example, suppose you focus sharply on your subject ten feet away. Then how can you tell how much of the picture will be in sharp focus in the foreground or the background? The simplest way is to look at the focusing scale on your camera. For example, if you are using a 55mm lens on your 35mm camera, your lens opening is set at f/8 and you are focused at ten feet, your distance scale will indicate that everything will be in sharp focus from eight and one-half to fourteen feet. This is the depth of field covered by that lens at that distance at that f stop.

You will also find on most expensive 35mm cameras a preview button. The lens is open while you focus. Then, by pressing this button, you will see in the viewfinder just what depth you will get at the exposure you have set. In practice this does not work too well—the eye cannot accurately judge just how sharp the foreground is nor just when the background will go out of focus. It is simpler to check the scale or just remember that if you want the background out of focus, you must use a large lens opening and a faster shutter speed. If you want an in-focus background (and foreground) use a small lens opening and a slower shutter speed. Speed and judgment in focusing comes with practice and experience. So try close-ups, medium and long shots and check the results.

5
FILMS, PROCESSING VIEWING AND CAPTIONING

ABOUT FILMS

The rules to remember about film are brief but important:

1. All film is dated. You will not get as good pictures on old film as on fresh film. Be sure to check the expiration date and never buy outdated, or even almost outdated, film.

2. Unless you are going to use the film immediately, keep the unexposed film in a cool, dry place. A refrigerator is a good place to store it, but be sure to use a plastic container with a tight cover. Thirty-five millimeter film comes in rolls of 20 or 36 exposures. Unless you are going to take a lot of pictures, the 20-exposure roll may be best for you. You pay a little more, but there is less chance of the film getting old in the camera or on the shelf.

3. After exposure, get the film out of the camera and to the processor as soon as possible. Extremes in temperature and moisture both affect undeveloped film. The worst thing you can do is leave the film in the camera and the camera in the glove compartment of your car or in a warm closet at home. This kind of treatment is almost sure to affect your transparencies or negatives.

4. Select a film that fits your needs (see film index) and, as far as possible, stick with it. This goes for both black and white and color. While there are films for all sorts of special purposes, it is much easier to take pictures with a film you are used to. This is true not only in 35mm film but in the 110 and 126 films for pocket-size cameras, and also for all instant film.

5. In 35mm and pocket-size films you will have to choose between color positive and color negative films. The color positive films, such as Kodachrome, result in a transparency for projection. You can also have

prints made from your positive transparencies but an inter-negative must be made and that costs a little more. Better prints usually come from negative color film. It is important, then, to decide which are more important to you—transparencies or prints. If you want both, positive color film is your only intelligent choice.

Black and white films come only in negative stock. From your black and white negatives you can have a contact sheet made which will show, in positive prints on one 8 x 10 sheet of paper, the entire roll of film. It is best to have this contact sheet made, then with a magnifying glass select the picture you wish enlarged.

ABOUT PROCESSING

To get the most out of your film, check up on your processor. Whether you use a drugstore or a commercial finishing laboratory, take the trouble to find out how good a job they do. In the case of the color positive films, such as Kodachrome and Ektachrome, you can specify that they be processed by Eastman Kodak; generally, this insures high quality processing. Eastman also processes color film for its pocket cameras. But if you are using film not processed by Eastman, or black and white film, try a few rolls first and check to see whether there are dust spots, water spots or scratches on your transparencies, color negatives or black and white negatives. Specify fine grain development for your black and white films. When the pictures are enlarged, the quality will be better.

If you are dealing with custom processing rather than mass processing, you can have your film speeded up. Suppose you are in a situation where there is not enough light. The ASA speed rating and the exposure indicator show that you cannot take acceptable pictures. It is possible, then, to underexpose, using a higher ASA speed, and then request that your processor overdevelop the film. This means he will develop it longer and you will get a relatively well-exposed negative, even though your meter indicated that there was not enough light. Such film always shows more grain. Professionals and advanced amateurs sometimes underexpose and overdevelop to purposely produce a grainy effect.

Let's assume you have space enough for a darkroom in your home or are willing to convert your bathroom into a part-time darkroom. You can develop your black and white film in a daylight developing tank that can be loaded in daylight, the developer poured in, the film agitated, the developer poured out, a stop bath poured in and out, a fixing bath poured in and out; then the top can be taken off and the film washed. But the temperature of your developing solution, and preferably the other solutions as well, must be kept at a recommended temperature. One way to do this in very hot climates is to cool a pan of water down to the proper temperature (or, in cold climates, raise it to the proper temperature), add the developing solution and, when it has reached the recommended developing temperature, proceed.

There is not much point in doing your own processing unless you are going to make your own prints as well. This means you will need a first-class enlarger which should be placed on a perfectly steady counter or table. To make a print the darkroom should have no light leaks. A red or amber safe light, which will not fog the sensitized paper you are using, will allow you to see well enough to work.

Take a sheet of unexposed enlarging paper and cut it into strips, putting the strips back into the box. After putting the film into the enlarger, focus carefully on the printing frame, using a focuser which magnifies the grain for exact focusing. Then turn off the enlarger light, place the strip of enlarging paper across the printing frame and expose, with a blank sheet of plain paper covering all except a portion of the paper for a minimum length of time. Move your covering paper down and expose the next section, and repeat this process until you have made four exposures. This test strip technique will save a lot of paper for, when it is processed, you can tell which one of the four exposures yielded the best print quality. Only then do you place your printing paper under the enlarger and make the exposure for the number of seconds indicated. A print exposure meter or indicator that works well for experienced printers can be purchased.

Now you are about half finished with your print. For sitting next to you, in a tray, is your developing solution, which you have either mixed yourself or bought as a pre-mixed solution and added water. The temperature of this solution is important. If it is too hot, the print develops too fast; if too cool, too slowly. Most chemical temperature recommendations would be between 65 and 70 degrees. Carefully slip your sensitized paper into the solution all at once with a sideways movement and then agitate it either with a pair of tongs or by rocking the developing tray. When it has reached the exact point that you think makes a good print (usually about 2-3 minutes), carefully lift it out with your tongs and put it into the next tray, containing a stop bath which stops the action of the developer. After a brief interval, move it into the third tray containing the hypo or fixing solution. From here it goes into a wash tray where the print should be washed for a minimum of 15-20 minutes in continuously flowing water.

Then you are ready to dry your print. Electric driers probably work best but, again, they are expensive and heat up the darkroom. Most amateurs put their prints between blotters or use a book of blotters. For mat finish prints, whether one uses glossy paper or not, the blotter system works fairly well, although prints are sometimes inclined to curl a bit. The other system, called ferrotyping, utilizes a large chrome metal sheet. The print is placed face forward against the chrome surface and a squeegee or sponge is used to extract the water and air bubbles. After a few hours, the print dries and falls off the chrome plate, leaving the print with a glossy surface. There is a small electric drier in which either glossy or mat prints can be made, one or two at a time. With this drier, the print is put against the shiny surface, squeegeed and then a cloth backing put over it and the heat turned on.

Every individual will find slightly different printing methods, and there are many excellent books devoted to black and white printing. Whether you develop and print your own black and white pictures or have them done by a laboratory is certainly a personal choice. But the author believes that the best processing, and usually the best printing, is done by professionals. On the whole, it is less expensive and more efficient.

It takes years to become an expert printer of black and white pictures. Most people never develop the knack. The equipment takes up considerable space, printing papers and chemicals must be kept on hand (they deteriorate fairly rapidly), and the process of drying negatives or prints is time-consuming and tedious. On the positive side, there is a great deal of creative satisfaction in taking pictures, developing them and, finally, making your own prints. But it is for the amateur with plenty of space, time and money to invest.

Color processing is more difficult and takes more special equipment than black and white. Because of time and temperature controls, professional finishing plants almost inevitably do a better job than the amateur. But even after having your color film processed and returned to you mounted and ready for viewing, what do you do with the pictures?

If you are using negative color film, it is simple enough to order standard size prints from the negatives you prefer. Many commercial processors will make an 8 x 10 contact sheet from your color negatives (not transparencies). A contact sheet should be filed with your color or black and white negatives in an 8 x 10 glassine envelope, preferably in a fireproof metal cabinet, for easy identification when you need additional prints. Then you will want some kind of filing system for your prints; either an album, which is probably the best way to keep them from getting lost or discarded, or a cardboard or metal box that can be labeled to identify scenics, portraits, action, children, etc. Based upon the kind of pictures you take, you will know best what kind of filing system you will need. But remember, if pictures are important enough to take, they are important enough to keep and to be able to locate when you want to view them.

Color transparencies are easier to handle than prints. As soon as they are returned they should be captioned. A few words on a self-adhesive label, handwritten or typed, and stuck onto the mount (being careful that the size of the caption does not exceed the size of the mount so that no edges are protruding) is easily the best technique. You will want some kind of metal file. Most camera stores handle simple metal files that take up to 100 slides or more.

ABOUT
VIEWING AND CAPTIONING

For a slide show (and it is great fun to please a select audience with your pictures), a good projector is important. A cheap one may tear up your slides if they get caught in the mechanism or it may overheat, causing the film emulsion to burn or buckle. So buy the best projector you can afford. It need not be fancy but it should operate smoothly, not overheat and be easy to load. If you are going to concentrate on 35mm slides (and they make up the overwhelmingly large proportion of color slides), you will naturally want a 35mm projector. It can also be used to project the slides from pocket cameras when the film is mounted in a 2 x 2″ cardboard adapter.

One of the most interesting new developments in slide projection is the use of two projectors connected and run in close sequence, so that one picture fades or dissolves into another. With this combination double slide equipment your sequences run almost as though you were looking at a motion picture without interruptions. If you are using a good camera and have taught yourself to take interesting color pictures, a little extra money invested in a good projector, or even two, is money well spent. Slides are not of much use when they are packed away and left in their yellow boxes with a rubber band around them.

Once you have decided upon your type of slide projector, consider each slide carefully before you show it publicly. Some type of light box upon which slides can be placed for viewing and editing is essential. Most of them are inexpensive and not very efficient. On the very cheap light boxes, the mounted transparencies are likely to slide off the plastic frame. This results in the slides getting scratched and picking up dirt. If you can possibly afford it (and you may have to ask your camera store to order it), invest in a good light box for editing your pictures.

When you edit and number slides, it is a good idea to put a red mark in the upper right-hand corner of the slide to show the top of it when it is in the machine. Slides go into most projectors upside down and with the dull side facing toward the screen. If you have your slides properly marked, you'll never get them into the projector upside down, sideways or backwards.

Once you have a tray of slides loaded, you may want to keep that tray ready for a showing at another time. If so, be sure to put it in a box—for trays full of slides are notorious dust collectors, and dust is the implacable enemy of film. When it adheres it is difficult to remove. Use a camel's hair brush and use it very carefully. Avoid touching the slide with your fingers. Oil from the skin is impossible to remove from film except by a professional finisher. In addition to being almost impossible to remove, the oil also gathers dust and not even the camel's hair brush will take it off. So either handle your slides by their edges or purchase a pair of inexpensive white gloves (professional finishers wear them when they are sorting slides) and use them when you are preparing your slides for projection.

Now about your screen. If you have a white wall in the living or dining room and can put your projector on a table, it saves a lot of trouble. Screens are unwieldy and even the best of them are inclined to pick up streaks, cracks and dirt. However, there may be no other choice. If that is the case, try to buy a good (and not too big) lenticular screen. Try out the stand that comes with it and see whether the screen material stretches evenly when it is opened ready for use. The advantage of this type of screen over beaded screens, mat screens and white walls is that, if you have viewers sitting on the side, they see the image with the same brightness as those seated in the center. Visibility on other types of viewing surfaces is likely to drop off as much as 50 percent for viewers sitting at a sharp angle.

Whether you are using your wall (which gives only fair overall brightness) or a good lenticular screen, it is important that the room be relatively dark. It need not be totally dark but it is best, if you use a light in the room, to have it shaded so that it does not reflect onto the screen.

Don't bother to buy a very large screen. If you are going to be asked by your camera club, high school or college to show your slides to a large group, let them supply the screen. For home use, you certainly need nothing larger than a four-foot square surface.

When you put together a show, keep in mind that the interests of your audience may not be similar to yours. And remember the old show business rule that you should never quite satisfy the audience. Always end your act with them wanting more. Informal, after-dinner slide shows should run about 20 minutes. If you really want to make a big thing of it, make it 30 minutes but have a break at the end of 15 minutes, and make the second half of your show different from the first. Nor should any slide be on the screen for more than a few seconds. Keep the show moving and keep your comments about each slide pertinent and brief.

A trial run is an absolute necessity before showing your slides publicly. If you want to keep your reputation as a good photographer, don't even take a chance on showing them to your wife, husband or housemate. Nothing reduces the image of the photographer in the viewer's eyes so much as seeing out-of-focus, upside down, or blank pictures on the screen. Your trial run will tell you that you should have your first slide in the machine, ready for projection when you turn the machine on. Otherwise you get a blinding glare that so enlarges the irises of the spectators that they are not likely to get a very good view of the first few slides. During your preparatory viewing, remove and replace all slides that you feel are not up to your standards—and be tough on yourself. Check out the focusing carefully on each one. If it is out of focus delete it.

Make a few notes regarding what you are going to say about each slide as it goes through the machine. Try to use some type of theme, even if it is only a chronological one showing the beginning and the end of a journey. There are many great themes. You may want to do an all-animal show, an all-miniature show, an all-flower show, a day at the beach, or at a carnival, the activities of a city, or the solitude and quiet that you thematized in a church sequence. By selecting a theme, you will not only interest your audience but will add a new dimension to your own creativity. You need not necessarily limit yourself to only one theme in a showing. Rather than one big feature sequence, it is sometimes better to do a series of short takes—perhaps 10 slides on one subject, then 10 on another. Selecting a theme, sequences and pictures is a highly individualistic enterprise. Let your presentation as well as your theme selection reflect your personality and sensitivity as a photographer.

6
PORTRAITS: FORMAL AND INFORMAL

A portrait is a way of remembering. It is a picture revealing a part of a person. You can never take a portrait that reveals the entire person. But you can take pictures that will show people the way they look to you. Each portrait contains two images, the one that the camera sees and records on film and the one that you, the photographer, see. The passport picture, for instance, with a blob of a head against a white background, is rarely revealing of the personality of the model. But when you take a picture you have the opportunity to see beyond the camera lens to add your impression of your friend, acquaintance, child, wife, husband or housemate.

Taking portraits should never be an ordeal for yourself or your model. The best way to avoid this is not to be insistent but rather to make it a mutually interesting session. There is no point in photographing someone who does not want to be photographed. Who wants such a picture? It is equally important for you to be relaxed and the best way to do this is to be sure you have thought out in advance what equipment you will need—you have the right film, you have decided on the lighting and the background, you have observed the model and you have some idea of how you want the portrait to look. Confidence on the part of the photographer is an absolute must. If you are nervous, can't find the lens shade or the film, your confusion is transmitted to your model and makes it difficult for the model to relax enough to fall into an easy pose.

In addition to having your equipment ready, there are a number of rules (although some should be broken at times) that will improve your portraits. Portraits, by definition, concentrate upon the subject's face, but you will find that including the model's hands, sometimes the shoulders and even the upper half of the body, will add great interest to the picture. Full figure portraits can also be interesting though the emphasis should still be on the subject's face.

Always stay far enough away from the subject so that the camera lens does not distort the face or be sure to use a medium long focus lens. The usual SLR 55mm lens is not ideal for portraiture. An 85mm, 90mm or

105mm lens will give better modeling and will not flatten out the nose. But it depends upon how serious you are about your pictures. If you are working with a pocket camera or a Polaroid, do not shoot at the closest possible distance the camera allows, but back away a couple of extra feet before making your exposure. The results will justify your caution. If necessary, you can crop the picture when you make an enlargement.

Backgrounds should be uncluttered. This is not always easy to achieve but, if you are working indoors with available light, a blank wall is ideal with the subject seated on a stool rather than slumped down in a chair. It is often necessary to take a picture off the wall to keep that distracting element from appearing in the background. If you want to give an impression of the type of person you are photographing by identifying something in the background, such as a bookcase, a large painting or a financial chart, it is usually best to focus carefully on the subject, using a large enough lens opening to be sure the background is well out of focus. This serves to separate the subject from the background.

If you are going to use black and white film, neutral pastel colors, which photograph in various shades of gray, are excellent. Black or white backgrounds are also effective. If you are making a color portrait, again, neutral backgrounds such as beige, black and white, are always effective, but soft pastel colors can be used as long as there is no color conflict with the subject. You would not want to use a redhead against a red background nor a black-haired person against a black background for the hair (unless strongly backlighted) will disappear. Remember that colors on either side of the model are reflected by the light so a room with green walls will produce a green cast, blue walls a blue cast, etc. So keep the model at least three feet away from a colorful wall or background.

Outdoor portraits should be taken in the shade or on an overcast day. The easiest and best way, in my opinion, is to pose the model outdoors against a solid color background—a wall, a hill, the side of a house—in the shade. You may want to throw the background out of focus. If your subject is seated on the grass, by shooting from a high angle the grass becomes an interesting background. But avoid splitting the head in half with the horizon line.

At the risk of being repetitious, I advise you to avoid portraits in direct sunlight—stick to open shade areas or an overcast sky when you're outdoors. And, when you're indoors, concentrate on light from windows, sliding doors or skylights.

We have mentioned filters in Chapter 4 but there are a series of filters that everyone who takes a serious portrait should know about. They are fog filters #1, #2, #3 and #4. They do not affect the sharpness of the picture unduly but they do diffuse the light over the film in such a way that wrinkles and skin blemishes can be reduced considerably, especially with #1 and #2. Filters #3 and #4 are likely to make your subjects look as though they are, indeed, in a fog, which is for some subjects not a bad idea at all.

A simple square reflector (some of them even fold up) can be purchased from any camera store and can almost double your amount of available light. When working indoors with an open door or window lighting the subject, put the reflector opposite the window and move it until you see the light reflected on the subject. A professional reflector is not an absolute necessity. A white towel stretched over the back of a chair is a fair substitute, though it does not throw as much light as a commercial reflector. The reflector can be used just as well outdoors as indoors, and will make your portraits look much more professional. It is especially useful when you are backlighting the subject with sunlight and then throwing soft light back onto the subject's face with your reflector. The reflector is placed near the camera and moved about until the lighting pleases you.

Avoid portraits with flashbulbs whenever possible. With the new films and lenses, flash is usually unnecessary for portraiture. It is effective to record a group of people at a party and you may want to make a record of an individual. But, because of the intensity of the light and because the light of most flash pictures is directed from the camera, modeling of the subject's face is lacking. You're very likely to come up with a picture showing startled, staring eyes, black holes where the nose should be and a hard etched mouth. But, if you do take flash portraits, back away to include at least head and shoulders. A portrait of two people taken with flash is more interesting than one because the camera and bulb are a little further away. Avoid reflective backgrounds that will throw a reflection directly back into the camera. Your model's glasses should be taken off or the head tilted downward which will keep the flash from reflecting in the lenses. If your camera allows it, use the flashcube in an extender or a detachable flash holder moved away from the camera lens, and remember that the distance from the subject is all important in flash exposure.

Now let's back up a little and look at the model that you are going to photograph. Check out a head-on view. Now try the model at a three-quarter view, an angle showing both eyes. First try the left side, then the right. Look at the model in profile. One side of the face may seem more interesting to you than the other. You may notice that few faces are truly symmetrical and usually one eye is slightly smaller than the other. Try to find a way that the model looks *right* to you, for the angle of the camera is important in portraiture. Most people can be photographed well with the camera an inch or two above their eye level. Yet there are many exceptions for, by raising the camera and tilting it downward slightly, a face can be elongated (if it seems too round) and the double chin or under chin lines are completely eliminated. A low angle will accentuate the chin.

Decide whether your portrait will be most revealing with the subject in repose or with an animated expression. The eyes do not always have to be looking at the lens. Often portraits are most effective with the subject looking off to one side or at the photographer rather than at the camera.

I mentioned the use of hands before. They can be used in many ways. One hand against the model's face may be effective or two hands may help to define the shape of the face. Some people smoke a lot and a cigarette or cigar often helps the model to relax and look natural. But, when you use the hands, be careful not to give the effect of amputating one of them or cutting too deeply into the shoulders. It is surprising how easy it is to cut into the shoulders, elbows, arms or hands and this can ruin the line of a well composed picture. Keep in mind that, by using the model's hands, you can make your male model look more masculine, your female model more feminine. If your female model's shoulders are too broad, use a dark blouse or a drape to cut them down.

Back to camera angles. Sometimes a slight lift of the chin will make the model look more self-assured. A smile in the eyes can often be more effective than a grin showing a lot of uneven teeth. Downcast eyes and a slight tilt downward of the face gives a pensive look. Try tilting the head of the model sideways. To be in control while the model moves about, it is a good idea to start with your lens level with the tip of your model's nose. This puts the lens in the center of the face so that when the face is tilted upward or downward or turned to one side or another, the same framing of the picture is maintained.

People are not always smiling nor are they always frowning, yet most people have characteristic expressions. By talking to the model you can sometimes catch a fleeting expression that makes for more than a routine portrait. Try to find a subject that interests your models and let them talk for a while, or surprise them with a comment that they least expect and watch for the reaction. Remember, too, that there are all kinds of smiles. Often a smile can be concentrated around the eyes with just the slightest hint of the upturned lips. Smiles are questioning, shy, happy, sexy, mysterious or mischievous. But don't overdo it. Remember that an expression of contentment or of dignity can sometimes best express the character of your model.

You'll find more about lighting for portraiture in the chapter on ARTIFICIAL LIGHT. It is enough to say here that there are two simple techniques: one is to bounce your flashbulb or strobe light off the ceiling. This gives the effect of available light. The second is to set up a small studio, use a simple background, a floodlight near the camera and slightly above it, and a modeling light closer and to the right or the left of the subject.

A good portrait should have the effect of depth, of being three-dimensional. Painters have known this for hundreds of years. As early as 1435, Alberti, in his treatise on painting, said:

"I say that learned and unlearned alike will praise those heads which appear to stand out from the picture as if they were sculptured."

Using the new techniques of a zoom lens, a prism supplementary lens and multiple exposure, this complex portrait shows seven images on one film. The zoom effect can best be seen in the small head visible within the larger one.

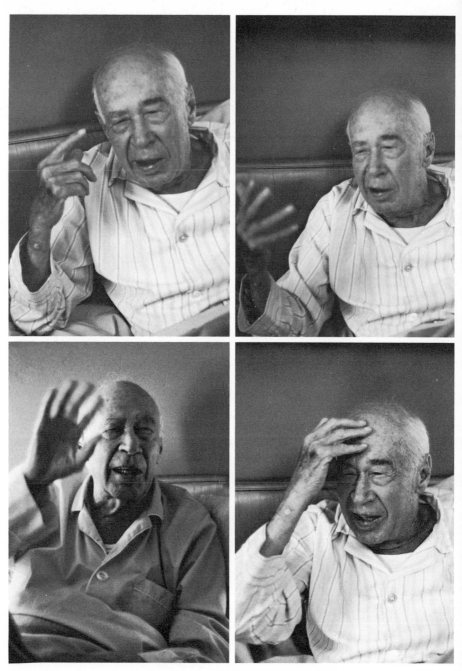

Candid portraits of author Henry Miller at the age of 84. In the midst of a bedside interview I propped my SLR camera against the doorframe and shot the entire sequence with an 85mm lens with fast film at 1/30 of a second.

An improvised formal portrait of the Spanish artist José Hernandez in his studio in Madrid. Chiaroscuro lighting produced by one photoflood lamp with unpainted framed canvas as a reflector. Camera on tripod, medium fast film.

The movement of the hands and rhythm of the pose show that this portrait was made while the fiddler was playing. Shutter speed was 1/30—enough to show the hands in motion but fast enough to keep heads of man and boy sharp.

Environmental portrait of legendary Dixieland jazz trumpet player Oscar "Papa" Celestin on the front steps of his modest New Orleans home. His awed listener is a grandchild. "Papa" was pouring out music as I released shutter.

Direct light illuminates every wrinkle and outlines the bone structure to show the character of this Tennessee mountain woman at an outdoor song festival. The log cabin in the background was purposely thrown out of focus.

62

Portrait of a Kentucky coal miner just home from work and before his bath. I posed his blond baby in his arms for contrast and used a large lens opening to put the other three children in the background out of focus.

While illustrating an article called "Mr. Citizen," later a book, I shot this picture as part of my "Truman in Independence" series. Relaxed informal group portrait shows former president Harry S. Truman with brother and

a friend on his brother's farm near Independence, Missouri. Late afternoon sun coming through the trees added to the natural effect. Concentrating on the dog, the group completely ignored the photographer.

Snapshot portrait of Mohandas Gandhi taken on a morning walk near New Delhi. This is a difficult picture, for the photographer must stop well ahead of the subject, focus on the zone or area and wait for subject to come into view.

An informal, but posed, portrait of Harry S. Truman. Truman, after a dawn walk, read the morning papers on the screen porch of his Independence home. Available light, shooting toward the sunlight to outline his profile.

The candid portrait. In the early morning Helen Keller was taking her morning walk. When she stopped for a moment to rest, she knelt and embraced her Seeing Eye dog. Camera was focused and exposure had been preset.

Sunup portrait of the blind, deaf and dumb multitalented Helen Keller. She is shown waiting for the first warm rays of the sun, which she could feel but could not see. Six a.m., summer day, available light, camera on tripod.

This quick candid portrait was possible because the camera was prefocused on the teapot and the exposure was programmed by the camera's exposure system. Because of the bright sun backlighting, a lens shade was essential.

An informal portrait of a Japanese patriarch taken in my favorite light—open shade on a bright day. Medium fast film was used with fine grain development. The light, out of focus background adds to the cheerfulness of the picture.

Indirect light bouncing up from the white sand beach on Jamaica's north shore gives a soft flesh tone and modeling to the face of actress Ursula Andress. I asked her to cover her mouth to bring out the sensuous beauty of her eyes.

Backlighted, available light snapshot was made at action peak with pocket size camera. Photographer posed mother and child; waited for right moment.

Posed portrait was effective because of the proximity and contrast between grandfather and grandchild. Soft backlight gives outlines to the two heads.

An overcast sky creates soft pastel colors. The V-shaped composition focuses the eye on the model. Palm tree fringe across top completes the design.

Sunlight and shadow, water, sand and overhead vines were carefully chosen to effectively photograph actress Ursula Andress while on location in Jamaica.

A documentary travel type photograph shows a South American family. The photographer has avoided having the people look directly at the camera.

In this snapshot three old drinking companions pose for the photographer. From left to right they are Ian Fleming, Noel Coward and Peter Quennell.

7
NUDES AND SEMI-NUDES

When photographers began picturing the nude, few of them had taken the trouble to study the varieties of nude models, graceful poses and fluid compositions of the great painters who had celebrated the nude for so many hundreds of years. Yet for generations aspiring painters had taken their blank canvases to museums and meticulously set about copying the old masters. While I do not recommend that photographers slavishly copy the great painters of the nude, I do recommend careful observation of their work. For in the great paintings are literally hundreds of lessons. Every possible kind of light has been explored—the soft, natural light of Fragonard, the hard shadows of Manet, the touchable flesh tones of Rubens and Renoir. So, before you start, give some thought to the portrayal of the nude in the past.

The nude in painting appeared in Egypt as early as 2000 years before Christ. But it was not until the time of the Greeks that both male and female nudes (male nudes predominantly) became the highest expression of beauty. In Greek art the nude body represented harmony and proportion. Sexiness, or the portrayal of the male or female as a sex object, did not yet exist. Thus, the photographer today can learn little about sensuous effects from Greek painting or sculpture, except perhaps by noting how effectively flowing draperies accentuated the semi-nude forms they both concealed and revealed.

After the decline of the Greeks and the Romans, the nude was proscribed by the Christian Church and vanished. Artists of the Middle Ages produced few nudes except for Adam and Eve, their genitalia carefully covered with their hands or with leaves. (They were usually seen reluctantly departing from the Garden of Eden with an Angel of Wrath, sword upraised, pursuing them.)

The flesh and blood nude, with her sensuality as well as her beauty, was born among artists of the Renaissance. Raphael, Michelangelo, Giorgione, Botticelli, Tinteretto and Titian painted women, and occasionally men, in warm glowing colors and attitudes that accentuated their sexuality. Indeed, Titian painted such frankly sensual women in such provocative positions that many were never publicly displayed.

But, although it was chiefly the Italians who glorified the female figure, the Germans, best represented by Hans Memling (who painted the first full figure nude in the Western world), Lucas Cranach, Albrecht Dürer and Hans Grien, were also painting their own versions of Eve and Venus. It was not long before the Dutch painters became equally interested. Most notable and most prolific of them were Peter Paul Rubens and Rembrandt, who painted nudes in a realistic style. In Spain, Diego Velázquez electrified the court by showing a nude from the rear while an angel held a mirror which reflected her face.

With the succeeding generations, the nude female figure became ever more seductive, and myriad were the ways that artists found to depict her. Jean-Honoré Fragonard saw her in pink and white flesh, well rounded yet delicate and romantic. Francois Boucher showed her as frankly sensual while Jean-Auguste Dominique Ingres painted classical nudes that exuded sex and warmth. Both Francisco Goya and Gustave Courbet brought a new realism revealing the nude frankly and directly. The 19th century was distinguished by such painters as Edgar Degas, who loved to paint women in and out of their bath; Toulouse Lautrec, who caricatured them; and Pierre Auguste Renoir and Edouard Manet, who made them live and breathe.

In the 20th century, almost every facet of woman has been explored in the nudes of Amedeo Modigliani, Pablo Picasso, Georges Rouault, Marc Chagall, Salvador Dali, Pierre Bonnard, Henri Matisse, Tom Wesselmann, Paul Delvaux, and the great master (or mistress) of the nude, the Frenchwoman Leonor Fini. But, while all of these European and American concepts were developing, the sensuous, seductive nude had long been known in the wall paintings, bas-reliefs and sculptures of India and the *shunga* and *ukiyo-e* drawings and wood-block prints of Japan.

One of the things common to painting and photography is the importance of the model. Without an interesting, cooperative model, your nude photographs have little chance of pleasing you or anyone else. The model does not have to be a great female beauty nor a handsome male, for many figure faults can be corrected with lighting and posing.

Most good photographs of nudes are carefully posed. By using light and shadow and effective camera angles, and by intently viewing the model, it is possible to bring out the best features of any figure. But just because the model is posed, the resulting picture need not be rigid, formal or frozen. One way to avoid this is to develop an easy working relationship. The model—man, woman or child—must have absolute confidence in the photographer. Otherwise, the model's uneasiness or insecurity is inevitably transferred to the lens which, to the model, represents the photographer.

So it is always best to have a preliminary talk before starting a nude photography session. Keep in mind that this is a book for the amateur photographer and, although by following the modeling tips given in the succeeding text the model could possibly become a professional, it is also written for the amateur model.

Jim Moran, the publicist, writer and photographer of *The Classic Woman* (an extraordinary book of nude photographs which he made with a Polaroid camera) introduces himself, puts on a phonograph record, possibly plays the guitar, offers the model a cup of tea and has found that, in the ensuing conversation, the model becomes more and more at ease. Of course, if you're dealing with a close friend, lover, wife or husband, the preliminary period may not be as long, but it is always necessary. No one can jump right out of their clothing and pose easily for the camera.

It is important to plan the photography session at least two hours ahead, because when photographing women it takes a considerable amount of time for the pressure lines of panties and/or bras around the torso to disappear. See that the model wears no underwear for at least two hours before you start taking pictures. After carefully preparing just this way, I once made the mistake of asking the model to sit down while I was loading film into the camera. Unfortunately, she chose a chair with a woven seat pattern.

Makeup can be used to cover blemishes and bikini marks. But it must be body makeup and should be applied slowly and carefully with a sponge or a spray can. It is possible to match skin tones for there are a variety of shades available. You will need two or three different shades if you intend to do a lot of nude photographs.

Now to find your model. A great many women and a considerable number of men are perfectly willing to pose nude for a friend but would not consider posing for a professional photographer. The Polaroid camera is ideal for this kind of session for it eliminates a third person being involved in the processing and allows the pictures to become a kind of game with two people playing. After taking the first shot, the photographer and model can view the result and benefit by seeing what changes should be made in the pose, the lighting and the background.

The best way to begin is to convince your friend that you're sincerely trying to take as good pictures as possible; that you need someone to help with the project and that they will be able to see the results of the pictures. But be careful. There is no point in becoming involved in photographing people who do not have some pride and admiration for their bodies. People who dislike their figures are not going to be cooperative models and, even if they are, you are unlikely to come up with good nudes.

Because the overwhelming percentage of nude photographs have been of women, few amateurs and not too many professionals have had experience in photographing nude men. Actually, the same general rules of posing, lighting and camera angles apply. The picture, whether of a female or a male nude, finally depends on what you want the camera to reveal.

Just as it is important for the eye to become familiar with a landscape or a still life before the picture is composed, time must be taken to view the nude model. It's best to do this by imagining the figure in your mind as being composed of four parts: the torso, the head, the arms and the legs. By considering the parts of the body separately and then, after becoming familiar with them, putting them together, the most effective use can be made of each area. So look intently at the outline of the figure. Put a light behind the subject so that in silhouette the total shape becomes apparent. Then decide what you want to express in the picture. Is it going to be a soft flowing pose or a sharp angular one? Do you want to concentrate on the model's torso, head and arms and leave the legs (because they are too thin or too heavy) in shadow? Do you want your figure to look longer than it really is? Or shorter? All of these questions can be answered by studying the model. Don't hurry to get the model into a pose. Try a profile view from the right and a profile from the left. Even a slight variation in the angle can improve or detract from the picture. You may want to get away from the old-fashioned "feminine" pose where the model puts her weight on one leg and crosses one knee slightly over the other, but it is a good pose to begin with.

Think in terms of a continuous body contour by drawing an imaginary line down from the head to the feet. By keeping this in mind and viewing the model head on, you can immediately see whether the shoulders are too wide and need to be angled slightly, whether the breasts are not prominent enough and need to be crosslighted, whether the hips seem too broad or the knees too knobby. There is no point in getting too technical about this. The most important thing is to concentrate long enough to know what your model's best features are (or worst, if you go in for grotesque pictures) and then begin posing and lighting.

While all this observation is going on, be sure that the model is comfortable, that the studio is warm enough, and that the lights are not kept on so long that the model becomes blinded or covered with perspiration. It's best to have the model wear a light robe, remove it when you're checking out the lines of the figure and your lighting, then slip back into it while you go about the essential camera arrangements and props.

Before you try artificial light in the studio, an ideal way to learn about photographing nudes is by using existing light. This means that you can sometimes create interesting pictures on a bright day in a well-lighted living room or bedroom, or, if you are fortunate enough to be able to find outdoor privacy, in a garden, courtyard, wooded area or on a private beach. Here, again, the general rule is to avoid sunlight. Soft, diffused light from an overcast sky or open shade gives enough contrast to the shadow areas. There are some exceptions but it takes an extraordinarily good figure to stand the glare of direct sunlight. Occasionally the sun's rays coming through an open window and illuminating part of the body can be very effective, but such high contrast photography can be considered after you have become advanced. In the beginning, simple, natural light (as shadowless as possible), indoors or out, will teach you a great deal about the photography of the figure. One important technical note should be remembered. There are flaws of one kind or another in almost every body and the soft nude treatment, especially when photographing women, is invariably more pleasing than a harsh treatment.

The way the light falls upon the model and the color of the light (warm or cool) has much to do with the effect in the final picture. When photographing in an outdoor shaded area, it is sometimes necessary to use a very light pink or yellow filter on the camera lens to keep the shadows in the flesh tones from becoming too blue or green. This is also true when using window or skylight illumination indoors. But, again, try it without the filter. Excellent nudes, looking exactly like they look to your eye, can be made without any filter at all.

There are four other filters that I highly recommend for nude photography. These are fog filters #1, #2, #3 and #4. Each one diffuses the light that strikes the film, softening and yet not blurring the outline of the figure. Numbers 1 and 2 are most useful because, in the finished transparency or print, shadows and wrinkles become softer and more pleasing. Numbers 3 and 4 give a much more misty effect and can be used to get a dreamlike quality into the picture. Unfortunately, these filters are usually available only for the 35mm or larger cameras but, if you are using any camera, it is possible to tape a filter in front of the lens.

In addition to the camera and daylight color film, if you are using natural daylight, a lightweight tripod and a cable release are essential to good nude photography. This is simply because the light is not particularly strong, and therefore the exposure of the film to the light must be longer. The tripod has an additional advantage. It gives the photographer time to study the pose through the camera lens or viewfinder. The cable release keeps the camera from being moved as the release button is pressed.

Nude photography by artificial light can be almost as simple as photography by daylight. With sensitive black and white film (a list is given in the appendix of the book) or with high speed tungsten color film (made especially for artificial light) the photographer can use normal room lighting. Floor lamps may have to be moved to improve both the composition and the lighting of the picture. Many photographers use only one light source and soften the shadows by placing a white sheet of cardboard at an angle so that the shadows are illuminated by the reflected light that strikes the cardboard. The main light source can be a simple reflector with a #1 or #2 photoflood bulb or, if daylight or Polaroid film is being used, a blue daylight type photoflood lamp. This gives a Rembrandtesque light quality to the photograph. If the photographer uses artificial light, and wishes to get the effect of natural daylight, the light can be bounced off a light-colored ceiling or wall, preferably white. (Otherwise, the color will be reflected onto the model; that is, a yellow surface will result in yellowish flesh tones and a green one in greenish flesh tones.)

Now that you've observed the model and selected his or her best features, decided on the lighting, selected your film and loaded your camera, it's time to do the actual posing. Don't take the first pose immediately. Give yourself time to see how the model looks in a series of poses and be sure you have some idea of how you want the picture to look on the film.

Here are a few checkpoints:

1. Have the pantyhose or stocking and bra lines completely disappeared?

2. Have you moved the model to the camera or the camera to the model so that blemishes and bad angles are modified or eliminated?

3. Is there enough light reflected upward so that the model does not have dark circles under her eyes?

4. Is the background simple and uncluttered so that the lines of the figure create the composition?

5. Are the legs and the feet kept at approximately the same distance from the camera as the torso? If they are too close to the camera, they will appear too large.

6. Never seat the model nor have the model lie on a textured or roughly woven material if you plan other poses afterward.

7. If the model is seated, be sure you're not shooting from an angle that flattens out the buttocks.

8. Talk to the model to keep her relaxed.

9. Take your time. Relax and enjoy the shooting.

The use of color such as in a bright pillow, an ottoman or a beanbag chair can add considerable interest in nude photography, but it is important to be careful not to let the color overpower the flesh tones of the model. It is a rare nude that can be photographed against a red background. Pastel colors in props and backgrounds are usually best. Try not to be too realistic, too direct, in photographing nudes. This is one reason why filters and pastel colors are helpful. Too much realism is likely to destroy the mood you have tried to achieve, in a soft bedroom scene or a quiet woodland setting.

But if you are going to photograph a nude surfer on the crest of a wave, or a nude dancer in the sunlight, or a nude swimmer with skin sparkling from the droplets of water and the shimmering green-blue background, then you will probably want to get all the sharpness and realism possible in the picture.

Actually, the swimming pool and the beach are two excellent settings for nude photographs. Shooting down from a diving board on a nude figure yields a most effective picture. These, of course, can be done in direct sunlight, but if you want the model's eyes open, be sure the sun is behind rather than directly above the head. Divers can be photographed in midair with an exposure of from 1/500 to 1/1000 of a second. This means you won't be able to stop the motion with a pocket-size camera nor with most Polaroid models. But it is easy with the SLR. In fact, an effective series can be made showing the diver on the board, in the air, just as the hands touch the water and then just as the feet disappear.

Comparatively inexpensive underwater housings for SLR cameras are available, and there are some waterproof 35mm cameras (not the reflex type, but those with a distance scale) with which excellent underwater nudes can be made in swimming pools or, if the water is clear, along the coastline. You need only a snorkel and mask and your camera, either in a housing or (if it is the underwater type) around your neck. Decide approximately at what distance you want to photograph, tell the model what to do underwater and in which direction to swim. Then you may tell the model to count to five, after you submerge, before diving. Take a deep breath and submerge to the depth you think would be best for the exposure. As the model swims down there is usually time for you to take at least two pictures before coming up for air. Lying on the surface with mask and snorkel, it is possible to photograph the model from above instead of at the same level or from below. It is important, however, that the water be crystal clear and the sun bright. Under these conditions, photographs of nudes are easy to take.

Back in the forties and fifties, some of the large processing plants practiced censorship; they refused to return films that depicted direct frontal nudes. Now, the nude has finally been universally accepted as respectable, so you need not worry about sending your nude photographs to Eastman for processing or to any other legitimate processing laboratory. Of course, this applies to both color and black and white negatives and prints. There may be some smaller local laboratories that exercise local option, but the labs in the larger cities treat nudes just as they do landscapes.

Photography, generally, is inclined to be truthful and photography of the nude is no exception. Indeed, it is difficult to romanticize or glamorize the nude as many artists do. The photographic nude at its best has a natural, unposed look. There is great natural beauty in the athletic body, male or female, in repose or in motion. The soft feminine figure, all curves and roundness, has its special kind of beauty. Camera technique, setting, composition and posing should always be compatible to the type of nude model being photographed. She can be frankly provocative as she poses or naive in front of the camera. Your pictures may express her modesty, her sensuality, her narcissism. You may see her, and represent her, as a tigress, a virgin, a goddess or the girl next door.

There was a time when all of us were nude—before animal skins or clothing were worn. Try to show the natural ease of the body unclothed in your outdoor nudes. You will find that the natural gesture and pose works best even with more sophisticated indoor nude photographs. Many important nudes in painting have been inspired by poetry, poetic prose and mythology. While I do not suggest that you photograph nudes as nymphs or mythological goddesses, I do suggest that great themes for modern photographic nudes can be inspired by poetry, past and present. The Eve of today offers an infinite variety for representation.

But, as I have suggested throughout this book: to be a good photographer, learn and observe the rules. Then, to be a great photographer, break them.

An outrageous wig and the colorful stockings (the color is noticeable even in this monotone photograph) tie this happy nude together. Lens was normal 55mm. Light was from an open door on the right and a portable reflector.

The white background and white chair accentuate the model's flesh tone. Her arms and legs complete a symmetrical, vertical pattern. By concealing the figure behind the heart-shaped chairback an element of mystery is added.

Available light from a large glass door was used without a reflector. An unposed effect was achieved by the heavy shadows and the relaxed, languid pose. Camera was placed on tripod for exposure of 1/30 of a second at f/2.

A good approach to photographing the nude is simplicity. Concentrate on the lines of the figure and separate the model from the background. The sculptural quality is as apparent in the female as in the male figure.

84

Candid nude caught young tourists washing before entering a public bath at the Ohashi Ryokan (inn) in Misasa, Japan. The light was very dim: a slow speed and wide open lens were necessary, which accounts for the slight movement.

Two 600-watt quartz floodlights were bounced off the ceiling to even the indoor and outdoor brightness. This test photo was made to show how a straight unfiltered picture differs from one where a filter is used.

A number 4 fog filter changed the mood of the picture completely. Instead of a naked girl in a room, we see a high-key dreamlike photograph. The exposure was only one-half stop more with the fog filter. Lighting was the same.

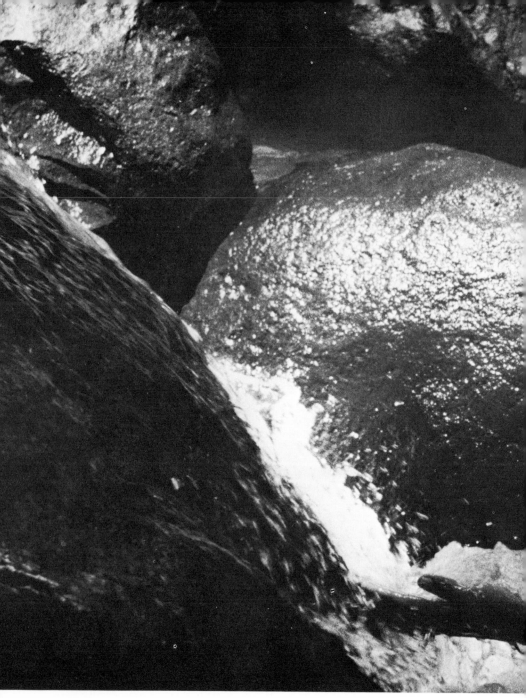

Bright sunlight reflects off the swift-running water and smooth rock surface of a secluded waterfall to illuminate this young Carib Indian girl (one of the last descendants of the fierce Caribs that Christopher Columbus battled and

described in the journals of his second voyage) bathing in a warm cascade on the remote West Indies island of Dominica. The print was made on a low contrast paper to offset the high contrast of sunlight and shadow of the scene.

Question: Where was the photographer? Answer: Almost directly over the model on the tip of the diving board. A wide angle 21mm lens was essential for this picture, for distance from photographer to model was only five feet.

I focused the camera and waited to surprise the subject when she surfaced. Spontaneity, action and water glistening and dripping were my aim. The bright sunlight did not keep model from opening her eyes when she saw the camera.

An action nude taken from the diving board just after the diver took off. I waited until just before her hands broke the water, then pressed the shutter. The lens had been prefocused. Exposure was 1/1000 of a second at f/8.

I shot the same diver from the opposite side of the pool at approximately the same moment of her entry into the water. This shot, because of the length of the pool, required a 200mm lens. Exposure was the same as in other picture.

Complex approach to photographing a nude is seen in this prism photograph. Such supplementary lenses are available at camera stores. They add variety to many types of photography. With most prism lenses the exposure remains normal.

A reflector was added to bounce the available light back onto the model. Telephones make good props and model was more at ease talking to a friend. Her hand is larger than it should be because it is too near the camera.

Voyeur photograph was taken through sparse pine tree branches as the unaware model pinned up her hair and prepared to sunbathe. A 200mm telephoto lens was focused on the model, causing tree branches in the foreground to blur.

The photographer is only a few feet under the water as the model swims toward him. The Nikonos camera was prefocused at 3 to 7 feet at f/5.6 at 1/250th.

A long line from the part in her hair down to her heel elongates the model's body with a bright light on her right side. Background enhances yoga theme.

Out of focus oranges and orange blossoms add interest to this summer nude portrait. Camera is focused on the face causing the out of focus foreground.

A 5′1″ girl becomes a tall model. Available light portrait was made with wide angle lens to extend the model's legs. Illumination is from glass door.

Double image of nude lying on a low window ledge creates an interesting available light composition. Leaves, bushes and grass are seen outside of windows.

8
STILL LIFE
AND
TABLE TOP

Still life is a relative term borrowed from artists who use it to describe the painting of personally arranged compositions of inanimate objects. In still life photography there are sometimes overlaps with nature and documentary picture taking. While all photographic work of interest requires creative effort, still life photographs push your imagination and technique to their outer limits. The photography of flowers and plants (arranged or in their natural state), of fruits and vegetables, of a leaf, a blade of grass, a rock—indeed, all inanimate objects—challenges any photograher, amateur or professional. Here there is no passing scene, no action, no interesting models to help make the photograph noteworthy. There is just you, your camera and the object, which is not going to smile at you.

As you look at a leaf, the pattern emerges when the eye observes and the mind records. The brain may interpret the pattern in many ways depending upon the meaning it makes out of the information that the eye has delivered. The pattern may be of a ladder, it may remind you of a religious symbol, such as a menorah or a series of crosses. What you perceive in the leaf you may want to emphasize in your picture of it. A rock may remind you of a head in profile. A single slice of tomato could be a wheel.

It is interesting for the photographer to allow his eye to wander over the object long enough to allow the mind to recognize the symbolic meaning within. Once you have recognized a symbol in the object and emphasized its meaning with light, other people viewing your photograph will understand your picture's meaning from the symbolism in it. You will have photographed an idea. The viewer may find meanings of his own within the picture you have created. An apple photographed with the lens of the camera even with it and a sky in the background can be symbolic of the universe. Thrust a small paring knife into it and the idea of destruction or violence emerges. Cut it in half or in quarters and it can become a symbol of reproduction.

How then to make this rock, this flower, this piece of sculpture reflect your creativity? First, there is the selection of the object itself. The very selection of it is an indication of your taste. After selection comes intense and considered observation. If it is an object that can be moved, the way the light falls upon it can be selected by you. If it is an object that cannot be moved, such as a large piece of sculpture, a tree, flowers in the garden, you must wait until the light is exactly as you want it. Then comes the angle of view. Is it the heart of the flower, one of its petals or the entire flower that you feel will make the most effective photograph? Is it the head or the curve of an arm or the muscles in the leg of the sculpture? Is it a box of tomatoes exposed at an outdoor market or a single tomato close up, backlighted by the sun? Or is it a portion of a single leaf showing the intricate leaf pattern that can be turned into an exciting abstract design in a black and white or color print?

An interesting example of the continuity that can be developed in still life photography is the work of a French photographer who for many years has selected vegetables, in the market, that are sexually symbolic. Some of them are fairly obvious, some very subtle. But there is an infinity of shapes in nature, and selection can run from purely abstract to hyper-real to romantic, humorous, dramatic or simplistic. The care of the fruits and vegetables you select can be as important as the selection itself. Edward Weston, perhaps the most famous of all still photographers, was always short of money and his children were always hungry. Each time he brought home bananas to photograph, he had to firmly instruct the children that the bananas were not to be eaten until after they were photographed. On at least one occasion it did not work out that way.

Still lifes are by no means limited to natural objects or art objects. It is possible to take an interesting picture of a chair, a piano (perhaps only a section of the black and white keys), a dressing table (with emphasis on the kind of objects upon it, to reveal the personality of its user).

But once the object has been selected, the lighting chosen and the point of view selected—what next? Interesting still life pictures can be made with many of the pocket-size cameras but, for the most part, the subject must be relatively large—a piece of sculpture or a portion of a flower garden—rather than the extreme close-up detail of a leaf for which this type of camera is not suited.

With the instant picture cameras, it is necessary to use a supplementary close-up lens for the smaller objects. More than usual care must be taken in making the exposure to insure the modeling effect and the lighting that you desire.

Rangefinder cameras can be used but, because rangefinders do not operate for extreme close-ups, they, too, are only useful for larger still lifes.

The SLR 35mm cameras, especially those with interchangeable lenses, are ideal for this type of photography. But regardless of which of these cameras you use, I highly recommend the use of a tripod and cable release for many reasons. It forces the viewer to look at the object longer without changing the angle of view, which is of great importance in still life photography. It allows you to use almost any kind of light, including dim light and long exposures, yet the resulting picture will be clear and sharp. There is an opportunity to use fine grain black and white films from which you can make mural-size enlargements that can become pleasing pictures for your walls. Slower color films, which allow more tonal gradation, can also be used when the camera is firmly supported and a cable release pressed gently. The cable release is used to keep from jarring the camera or tripod during the exposure. Finger pressure can be disastrous.

Another form of still life photography of importance to all amateurs is copying. I do not recommend that copying be done with pocket-size cameras. The resulting negative is too small in most cases, though there are exceptions. But with almost all 35mm cameras, a supplementary lens, an extension tube fitted to the regular lens, or a macro lens (which I recommend most highly), you can copy drawings, sketches, manuscripts, paintings and photographs, old or new. Copying takes concentration as well as proper selection of film and lights. If the job is done well, it is possible to make a copy that comes very close to the original. Copies can be made on either black and white or color film. Data sheets at the end of the book give information on slow films for copying.

While photographs can be copied in open shade or light from an overcast sky outdoors, more control is possible if they are mounted on a flat surface (they can be thumbtacked) or they can be placed on a home-made or an artist's easel. The camera should be on a tripod. Automatic cameras will give a reading, or it is easy enough to take a reading with an exposure meter. Professionals take the reading from the reflected light on a gray card which is available at your camera store. You will be most successful working indoors with two 3200K lamps in reflectors with the camera directly in front of the material to be copied. The lamps should be placed at a 45 degree angle from the center of the original. When working with a 35mm camera for copying, a fine grain film should be used (see data). These 3200K lights are ideal for color copying as well as black and white. As large an image as possible should be seen in your viewfinder to insure detail in the material you are copying. Should you want to do a great deal of copying, manufacturers make a special stand for the 35mm camera, complete with lights mounted at a 45 degree angle. This makes copying a pleasure.

A word of warning on certain legal restrictions having to do with copying. It is illegal to make copies of material bearing a copyright notice. This, of course, does not refer to old photographs that you may own or that were taken more than 56 years ago, since their copyrights have expired and the material has come into the public domain. You may not legally copy such things as drivers' licenses, passports, immigration papers, paper currency, bonds and similar material. Should you want to copy U.S. postage stamps, they can be copied for stamp collection purposes, but the reproduction must be in black and white only and it must be less than two-thirds or more than one and a half times the size of the original stamp. Do not worry about copying U.S. or foreign coins. It is entirely legal to photograph them.

This is by no means a detailed account of the necessary materials and procedures for expert copying, but it covers the basic information. There are many books and pamphlets on copying available. It is usually better to have a processing company make copies of your color transparencies than to make them yourself—it's usually cheaper too.

The term *table top* has become archaic but the photography of small objects and the creation of miniature scenes to be photographed on a table top is an important way to take pictures. This kind of photography generally uses the same disciplines as still life photography described above. The biggest difference is that you may create an entire world of your own on a corner of a table. A mirror may become the sea; shadows can create a ship sailing on it. It is excellent practice for the amateur to take various objects, miniature pieces of sculpture or a bonsai garden, and note the light and shadow, the perspective and the exposure and make a picture recreating the scene. Much can be learned by emphasizing the size of one object compared to another, and the contrast created by adding or subtracting light from the scene. It is a great way to become familiar with the viewfinder. A few practice sessions with some table top objects can take the edge off of being afraid to use a new camera. At the same time, it will show the beginning photographer what the camera can do under controlled conditions.

The use of a table top with a camera on a tripod gives the amateur the idea of how commercial photographs of products are made. Try photographing a bottle. It will take quite a while to learn how to keep the lines of the bottle straight, how to control the reflections, what will be the best angle from which to show the product. Almost anything can be used for practice either for black and white pictures or for color. By using a small doll, some tinsel, a calling card or other recognizable objects it is possible to create effective Christmas cards or announcements with your camera.

Table top opportunities are limited only by the imagination of the photographer.

The end of a plantation house on the Mississippi River. Two huge columns had fallen and had begun to sink into the soft earth. In addition to being a still life and a landscape, this is also a documentary photograph.

In the Chapel of Miracles at St. Roch Church in New Orleans, I photographed a corner of the shrine. Over the years the sick and lame believers had come to be cured and many had left their crutches and braces. Camera on a tripod.

A piece of badly burned marble sculpture lay in the rubble in the aftermath of a volcanic eruption in Martinique. Exotic plants had grown up all around it. The light was dim but bright enough for a 1/60 of a second exposure at f/2.8.

By placing this small Mexican figurine of an ancient ballplayer on a large sheet of white seamless paper and curving it upward behind it as a background, shadows were avoided. Normal lens, two 600-watt quartz lights.

This early Mexican ballplayer, ball in hand, was also photographed on white background. Museum cooperation is essential for this type of photography, as well as care in light arrangement, positioning figurine and exposure.

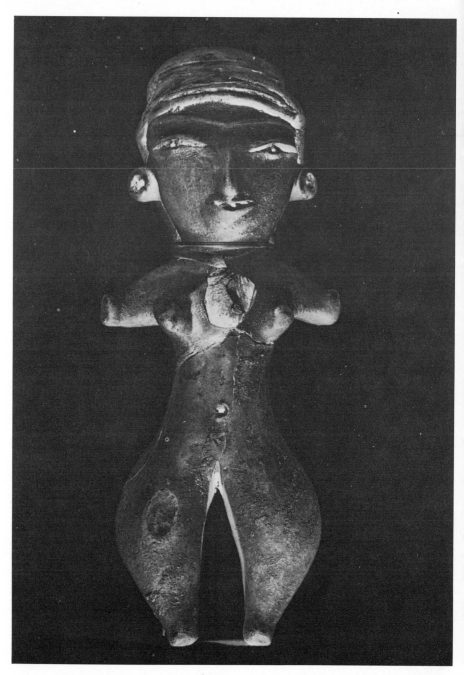

In this instance the use of the negative image was more effective than the positive. This reverse print was made from a 35mm positive color transparency. It is of an Olmec female figurine fashioned in Mexico before the time of Christ.

It took backlighting and sidelighting to bring out the detail of this minia-
ture sculpture by the French surrealist artist Jean Benoit. I used an SLR
35mm camera, macro lens and three 3200K floodlights in reflectors.

A diorama representing the landing of the first colonists at Jamestown, Virginia, on May 14, 1607. This picture was made by taking a time exposure with the camera on a tripod and utilizing the available diorama lighting.

At sunset, I climbed a scaffold to photograph in silhouette this statue of Captain John Smith, beloved of Pocahontas and defender of the Jamestown Colony, as he gazed out over the broad James River. A K2 filter, medium fast film, 55mm lens.

Composition made up of memorabilia from Lincoln's presidential campaign of 1860. Senator Hamlin was an ex-democrat. Lincoln's stand on slavery is expressed by his copy of Uncle Tom's Cabin. *Handbill, top hat and cane completed arrangement.*

This still life shows the sword, the felt hat, and leather gauntlets of Confederate General Robert E. Lee, photographed against his battle flag. Lighting was from two floodlights. This print was made from color transparency.

In this still life composition I arranged the surveying instruments, watch, snuffbox and dental instruments of George Washington. The objects were placed on the floor on a piece of his original carpeting (note the stars).

Reflected in a small pool is the magnificent Thomas Jefferson home, Monticello, near Charlottesville, Virginia. A tripod was necessary because the great depth of field made a long exposure necessary. Medium fast film at 1/2 second, f/22.

A perfect example of the kind of soft light that an overcast day provides. I climbed on top of my car, turned the camera to a vertical position to avoid distortion and then cropped some of the foreground out of the print.

It is difficult to put photographs into categories. This one could qualify as architectural. The scene is twilight, my favorite time for taking pictures, at Jackson Square in New Orleans. The church: Saint Louis Cathedral.

I viewed this quiet scene as a still life. There was not a ripple on the water, no one at home in the house. The late afternoon sun threw long shadows. I photographed from a grassy hummock using medium fast film.

9
THE TRAVELING CAMERA

The traveling camera leads two lives. It is with you to stimulate your viewing of myriad wonders as you travel, and it plays a permanent part in your life by allowing you to re-experience the pleasures of your journey. So, to make a trip a permanently pleasant experience, it is good to record those scenes that appeal to you with a camera. You will find that the kind of camera that travels best is relatively lightweight, uses a standard film size which can be purchased widely throughout the world, and will produce the kind of pictures that you want to stimulate your memory when you return home. Whether you make prints for your wall, your album or your friends or whether you elect to bring back transparencies, there are many cameras at many prices that travel well. Here are a few of the checkpoints.

Weight is important, for there is no use making interesting walking tours, climbing volcanoes, visiting natural and man-made wonders if carrying your camera is going to be a burden. But your choice is limited by the importance you put upon the pictures you take. All cameras, from the pocket-size, relatively inexpensive type on through the rangefinder and SLR cameras, are fairly small, and they range from featherweight to comparatively heavyweight. You will take better pictures with the SLR or the rangefinder 35mm types but, if you are going to take your travel photography seriously and want to do more than just record the passing scene, then the added weight of these cameras will not matter to you at all. However, don't forget that you will be carrying a half pound to two pounds two ounces of camera on a strap over your shoulder. Many travelers find it exciting to take along their 35mm camera with at least two supplementary lenses, a wide angle and a telephoto. I would be inclined to recommend, however, the medium zoom lens (see LENSES) which ranges from slightly wide angle to medium telephoto.

One of the advantages of the zoom lens when traveling is that it enables you, by using it at its telephoto extension, to stay well away from the subject. Most people do not like to be photographed and most pictures of people being photographed when they do not like it are highly unsatisfactory. In some cases, it may even mean the roughing up of the photographer. So, if your plan is to take scenes of native markets or bazaars, flower vendors, street entertainers, and indeed any pictures of which the models will be unaware, it is a good policy to have a lens that will allow you to photograph from some distance away. Most of the pocket cameras will not allow this, though there are occasional exceptions where a telephoto lens can be put into position on a pocket camera. The advantages of using the telephoto or semi-telephoto, that is, from 86mm to 200mm, are obvious. The photographer remains inconspicuous, the action is close up, and it is even possible to take portraits from a distance. So seriously consider one of the three zoom lenses previously described.

There are hazards attached to the heavier camera, too. For, even though insurance is a must, if you lose the camera or have it stolen, you have lost your opportunity to record your trip. These problems do not exist with the pocket-size type. You hardly notice the weight because it is in your pocket; you are unlikely to lose it and, if you do, it is easily replaceable. The pocket-size type means a smaller transparency to be used in a smaller projector to view a smaller image. But if the average television size image is adequate for you to project at home (and why not?) then the small size color transparencies work very well. If you use negative color film in these sub-miniature types, standard small prints, 3½ x 3½ and 3½ x 4½, are adequate to pass around and even to mount in an album. But you will not be able to produce big enlargements nor project large transparencies. There will always be some close-up and far away pictures that the pocket-size camera cannot handle—but it's a carefree, inexpensive way to go.

However, if you are not going to take your travel photography lightly, if you want to bring back larger films of your sojourns or safaris, I highly recommend the 35mm cameras. You may want to show your pictures at the local camera clubs; you may even want to sell them, for there is a good market for travel pictures.

When you travel, remember that your camera records an extension of your taste. Try for more than the documentary record. Attempt to get some of the way you feel about the trip into your pictures. There are many ways of doing this. One of the best is to develop a theme. A simple one might be "out of my window." Try taking the most interesting angle out of your window at dawn or, if it is more effective, at dusk. If you have a semi-telephoto, you may be able to get some of the life passing by in the street below you. If you are going to a number of cities, villages or parks, be sure to take at least three pictures from different angles at different times of day out of your window. You'll find yourself with a story having some kind of continuity and the visual impact of seeing these pictures in sequence will be surprisingly effective.

Perhaps music interests you. There is usually a shrine of some kind to an important musician in most large cities and in many villages in Europe. Follow Mozart around Salzburg and Vienna, or Grieg around Norway. If you are on a literary kick, consider the trail of Goethe in Frankfurt, Germany; photograph Shakespeare's England or Gertrude Stein's Paris. There are a thousand themes that range from pioneers to space travel.

There will be particular moments that you will want to relive and they can be recorded with any type of camera. I would not recommend black and white film, however, for generally it is the color, whether the tones be muted pastels or brilliant primaries, that will evoke memories most vividly.

The traveling camera can be very much at home in museums all over the world. Most museums allow the use of hand cameras. Pictures with flashbulb, flash cube or strobe lights are not allowed. For one thing, flashbulbs have been known to shatter, damaging a valuable painting. There is an even better reason. Flash pictures of paintings are a waste of film because, with the flash mounted on the camera, a reflection appears in the center of the painting which completely ruins the photograph. Because you cannot use flash, the 35mm camera with a reasonably fast lens, f/2 or larger, is a must. You simply do not have enough available light for the inexpensive pocket type cameras or the Polaroid types. You are better off with an automatic exposure type SLR. Because the light level will be fairly low and usually closer to daylight than artificial light, medium fast (ASA 64) to very fast (ASA 160) daylight film yields fairly good results. Sculpture is especially easy to shoot and paintings (depending upon how they are lighted) come off fairly well.

Experienced photographers usually make a preliminary trip through the museum to determine the quality of the light and then decide which film is best. If the paintings are entirely lighted with tungsten (artificial light), then tungsten type or type B color film is indicated. Keep in mind that you may only want to make photographs to remind you of the museum and that you can purchase excellent slides at the museum of the paintings you want to project.

Churches offer some of the same problems as museums. But it is usually possible to photograph stained glass windows and even altars by using the largest possible lens opening that your camera has, steadying the camera on a church pew or against a column and then making the exposure.

To take memorable travel pictures it is often necessary to be up early. Waterfront scenes are particularly exciting as the fishermen return with their catch and ships begin unloading; the activity is greater then than at any other time of day. Avoid the hours between 10 AM and 2 PM—it's a good time for your siesta and a poor time for pictures.

Late afternoon is also a good time for travel pictures, and a good time to break the rules. Use silhouetted scenes, backlighted flower markets, long shadows over warm landscapes. What about after dark? Modern color films and modern cameras do make it possible to photograph brightly lighted streets, carnivals and theater marquees.

Indoors there is enough light without flash to record circuses, baseball, football and hockey games. But do not try to use flash at any of these events. The action is always too far away for the strobe or flashbulb to reach and you will waste your film. Most inexpensive pocket cameras do not have fast enough lenses for this type of photography. But the SLRs and the rangefinder types, with fast tungsten film and relatively slow exposures, will yield interesting transparencies and prints. There is one big *but*. You must select moments when the action is fairly slow or stopped. A fast skater, a running quarterback, cannot be completely stopped using natural light. But when there is a pileup of players or when a skater stops dramatically for a moment, that is the time carefully, without jarring the camera, to press the exposure button.

Careful planning is an important part of travel photography. If you are carrying a moderately expensive or expensive camera, it is best to register it with customs when you leave the U.S. This procedure takes only a few minutes and there is a customs office in every airport or ship docking area. The officer will give you a form upon which you will write the name of the camera, its serial number and its lens number. This means you will have no trouble getting it back into the country when you return.

Customs officers in foreign countries expect tourists to be carrying cameras with them and pose no problems unless the traveler is carrying an excessive amount of film. However, I have found that as many as 30 rolls of film (which, if they are 36 exposure rolls, will yield 1080 pictures, which should be enough for most trips) will not be questioned. It is a good plan to include some type B (tungsten) film along with the daylight for night scenes in color can be very effective.

If you are taking a lot of equipment and you plan to ship some or all of it with your luggage, you will need a lightweight metal carrying case lined with foam rubber. If you are going to carry the camera, lenses and film with you on the plane, boat or in your car, take the following precautions. Purchase a lightweight camera bag—cloth or plastic is usually lighter than leather and it is possible to get waterproof types. Game bags used for hunting made of waterproof canvas and with a waterproof lining make excellent carrying cases. Many offered by manufacturers weigh more than the camera and double the load on your shoulder and the strain on your neck.

I have found it safe enough to ship my film in my regular suitcases (or in a metal case) but, after exposing it, it no longer can be sealed tightly and it is therefore better to keep it with me. For film deteriorates rapidly in heat, and by keeping it handy you can keep it in a relatively cool place. Never, never, leave it in the trunk of your car, where heat accumulates just as it does in the glove compartment. In either place your film can be ruined in hot weather. So far as possible, your film should be kept in a cool, dry place and, if you buy it some time before traveling, the refrigerator is a good place to store it. I have found that, unless the trip is going to be more than a month, it is much better to bring back film to be processed rather than have it processed on location.

Film must be kept dry and, on travel and vacations, many situations arise where this becomes a problem. On a rafting trip or a fast speedboat there is a good chance of spray hitting the exposed film you are carrying. You might even be drenched by a tropical cloudburst or forced to ford a stream. Normal film packing is not sufficient to keep film waterproof if the container becomes completely saturated or immersed. One sure way to keep the film bone dry—and I recommend it if you know you are going to be in a very wet environment—is to put each roll first back into its original plastic container (if you still have it) and then into a rubber contraceptive, tying a simple knot in the end. This completely waterproofs it.

One final travel tip: Keep a notebook handy and write a brief description of the scene when you shoot it whenever possible. It is altogether too easy to have a picture of a cathedral door and no idea of where the cathedral is located. Or to be projecting a magnificent waterfront scene and find that you can't remember in which country it is.

If you keep all the checkpoints above in mind, you will come back from each journey with interesting, printable or projectable pictures that will enable you to relive each moment.

The blessing of the hounds preceded this fox hunt near Warrenton, Virginia. Rain was beginning to fall. I composed the picture featuring the dogs in the foreground. To get greater depth I stopped the lens down to f/8.

In photographing Appalachia country, I came upon this poor family standing in their doorway. I sent a friend with whom I was traveling off to my left to attract their attention, then quickly framed and shot the picture.

A grandmother weaves a waterproof basket while her grandchild plays with a gourd. They are Carib Indians of Dominica, West Indies. I took two pictures with my Polaroid and gave them the first one in return for their cooperation.

A young black girl posed for me on the Caribbean Island of St. Vincent. On her head she carries a basket filled with sea-island cotton. I waited until she turned her eyes away from the sun to keep her from frowning into the camera.

Bright sunlight and shadow ("sol y sombre," as the Spanish say) make this photograph of bulls waiting to enter the arena realistic. The picture also shows the extreme range of light that is covered by modern black and white film.

A bull that would not die is shown on its knees in Mexican corrida. I had been following the action when the matador thrust in the sword but missed the heart. Final shot was made as he prepared a thrust into the brain.

While photographing an anthropological dig at the site where Columbus set up his first trading post on the northern coast of Hispaniola in December, 1492, I had to cross this shallow river. There, I watched and photographed Haitian

women fording the river, resembling an ancient biblical scene with their heavily laden donkeys. I stayed well out of sight and recorded the scene with a 200mm telephoto lens in order to avoid disturbing the subjects.

The ecstasy of voodoo devotees is shown in this single flashbulb picture. All were dancing forward. They were stopped by the 1/250-of-a-second synchronized flash. Overexposure compensates for the black skins and dark walls.

In a Japanese "ryokan," or inn, in Kyoto the attendant lowers the bamboo curtains after making up the "futon" (bed) for the night. Picture was posed with camera on tripod. Exposure with available light was 1/10 of a second.

This is not Africa but New Orleans at carnival time, and the Zulu king is arriving for the Mardi Gras. I was up at dawn. I managed to be one of the first to greet the king with camera ready. A K2 filter to darken the sky.

A mood picture taken in the late afternoon in Chesapeake Bay, Maryland. A fishing boat heads home. Heavy rain clouds obscure the sun yet there is enough reflected light on the water to silhouette both boat and fishermen.

Travel pictures do not always have to be of pretty scenes. Using single flash bulb on my 35mm rangefinder type camera made it possible to effectively record this tragic documentary-travel type picture of child labor in India.

In the Kentucky hill country, young singers perform at an outdoor folk festival. This simple snapshot depended upon the photographer waiting until light and action combined to concentrate the interest on the central figure.

One of the earliest Spanish missions in the West near Tubac, Arizona. A medium red filter made the scene dramatic. The camera was well away from the building to prevent distortion. Medium fast film. A brilliant sunlit day.

Wide angle lens makes giants of foreground sculpture and dwarfs the background buildings. The exposure was for the sky color, silhouetting the figures.

Night view from a motel room in San Francisco was made with a 50mm lens on 35mm camera braced on the windowsill. The exposure was one second at f/2.

Sunlight on the blue Caribbean water brings out detail of sailing vessel. Picture was taken with pocket type camera to show a small boat on a vast sea.

Out of a hotel window in Florence, Italy, with camera braced against the windowsill. Note how street lights help to establish the mood of the scene.

The quiet darkness of the interior of the cathedral is effectively seen in this available light one second exposure. Camera was braced on church pew.

The volleyball is high enough to accentuate Rio's Sugar Loaf Mountain. Late afternoon shadows and silhouetted figures create an unusual travel picture.

Close-up of hippo family was made with semi-telephoto 85mm lens from a river-boat. Cloudy sky made a low contrast portrait possible bringing out detail.

As I sat over a rum punch on Grand Turk Island, I saw this unique and amusing travel picture. With no time to compose, I focused and shot with my pocket camera. Later I found it was a man moving his restaurant down the beach.

10
ARTIFICIAL LIGHT

Only in recent years has the photographer had sufficient light to photograph any type of scene anywhere in the world at any time of day or night. For almost a hundred years following the taking of the first photograph, there was a problem of insufficient light. Four factors contributed to the solution of that problem. Films became more sensitive. Lenses were developed that admitted more light. Shutters were perfected to control light. But the most important factor was the development of new sources of light. Early solutions to the problem included hot, heavyweight incandescent studio floodlights. The heat was almost unbearable and the brightness intimidated models. It is true that these lights made studio portraits possible, but they did nothing to expand the areas in which photographers could work. Where the light was dim or nonexistent, photography remained impossible.

Then, in 1867, Timothy H. O'Sullivan, who had learned his trade as one of the most adventurous of the Civil War photographers, made a precedent-shattering series of pictures deep within the Comstock Lode mines near Virginia City, Nevada. In darkness, far below the surface of the earth, he set his camera on a tripod, loaded his film, took the cap off the lens of his camera and then ignited a quantity of magnesium which flared to produce a brilliant, penetrating light. His photographs were remarkable for these were scenes that had been previously believed to be unphotographable.

From Germany came *Blitzlichtpulver*, flash powder, which was a mixture of potassium chlorate, antimony sulphide and powdered magnesium. When it was ignited, it burned with an intense explosive flash and illuminated enough area to produce excellent black and white negatives when carefully used. Many of the early documentarians such as Jacob Riis and Lewis Hine exposed life in the tenements and sweatshops of the New York ghetto by using flash powder and the same open flash technique as O'Sullivan.

Control with flash powder was difficult. The photographer had to estimate distances carefully, be sure he did not use too much or too little powder and open or close the diaphragm of the lens (called *stopping down the lens*) to regulate exposure. It was a hazardous technique. I can remember a newspaper photographer friend of mine who decided to light up a large portion of Canal Street in New Orleans at night to record one of the Mardi Gras parades. He built a small scaffold for his tripod, waited until the parade reached his viewpoint, set a triple charge of powder in his hand-held flare holder, opened the shutter, fired the flashgun and blew himself right off the platform. He recovered from his broken leg in a few months and it took almost that long for his eyebrows and moustache to grow back. The picture turned out quite well: it ran on the first page of the *New Orleans Item*.

One cannot help but notice, in many of the famous documentary pictures taken with flash powder, between 1900 and 1925, the startled and sometimes even terrified expressions on the faces of factory workers, child laborers and miners. It is not surprising, for photographers often had to work in relative darkness; then, often when the subject least expected it, the explosion went off. Fortunately, more and more control became possible as German ingenuity again came up with a safer, more effective portable light source. It was a flash almost as bright as sunlight, created by an aluminum foil inside a glass bulb, ignited by means of battery-powered electric current. The flashgun gave the photographer much more control and the light was soon synchronized to the shutter so that the camera could be hand held. Batteries became smaller and more powerful; reflectors became more efficient. From this beginning came the flash cubes, flash bars and a whole assortment of flashbulbs now in use. When the camera release is pressed, a battery contact is made inside the camera, the shutter opened, the flash activated and the shutter closed. These small but powerful light sources have made artificial light so portable that pictures can be taken literally anywhere. Yet there is one disadvantage, the same one the original flash powder had. Because it must be attached, or very close, to the camera, the lighting is flat, there is little modeling in faces and backgrounds tend to be dark except when they are close to the subject.

There are two ways out of this dilemma. Some cameras, including the inexpensive pocket type, have a flash extension holder that moves the bulb a few more inches away from the lens. This helps a little but not much. Some flash holders allow the flash to be tilted upward and bounced off the ceiling instead of pointed directly at the subject. And it is possible to diffuse the light very effectively when there is a low, light-colored ceiling available. This does increase the exposure considerably, however, and can be used only after a great deal of experience with flashbulbs.

By the thirties and forties photographers were using multiple flash equipment. These were relatively large flashbulbs with reflectors that could be mounted on tripods and the light directed simultaneously from a number of different angles. After arranging the lighting, the photographer could set off all the flashbulbs at the same time fully illuminating a fairly large area. A "long peak" flash was developed. This type of light made it possible for the photographer to synchronize the lens, which was open for only a very brief period, with the peak of the light.

The first artificial light pictures showing dancers and ice skaters moving through the air were made with this equipment. It was tedious, dangerous work, for the bulbs had to be changed after every exposure, and the electrical contacts were often closed when they should have been open. Many a photographer working under pressure had a white-hot flashbulb go off in the palm of his hand while changing bulbs. It is an unforgettable and unpleasant experience. Yet he was better off than the earlier photographer using flash powder.

The small flash cubes and flashbulbs that are in use today are reasonably safe (yet they too have been known to shatter occasionally) and practical. They give adequate light for the kind of photography for which they are designed. They are especially useful with the pocket and Polaroid cameras, which almost always come equipped for flashbulb, flash-cube or flash-bar use. Instructions for use are simple and easy to follow. Yet many people find it difficult to make flawless flash pictures with good color values.

It is most important to remember that a good exposure usually depends upon the distance between you and your subject. (There are some exceptions with new Polaroid types.) With the most inexpensive type of pocket camera, which has no variable lens opening, the ideal distance is from five to eight feet. Even this range means that you will get more light on your subject at five feet and not enough at eight feet, depending upon the color of the walls of the room and of the background. By trial and error you may find that somewhere between six and seven feet is the ideal distance. The more expensive pocket-size cameras have lens openings that are adjustable, so that flash pictures can be taken either close up or at an average distance. My best advice is to carefully follow the instructions and make notes of your experiments until you know just how to get your best flashbulb effects.

Amateur photographers waste literally thousands of flashbulbs along with an equal amount of expensive film by taking pictures for which flashbulbs are completely unsuited. Sporting events, such as artificially lit baseball, basketball and hockey games, theatrical productions, high school and college entertainment, cannot be photographed with the small flashbulbs from the audience. The action is always too distant; the light from your flash cannot possibly carry far enough to expose the picture. All those annoying little flashes that are seen at various types of sports and entertainment events are a complete waste. Your film will be blank. Many of these events are so well lit that pictures can sometimes be taken without flash. But the bulb itself does not help. One gets the impression that many amateurs who use simple cameras with flashbulbs refuse to read or are unable to comprehend the simple instructions that come with the film. I have seen flash cubes in use at a football game in bright daylight. People even try to take flash pictures out of airplanes, where the light from the flash would have to reach thousands of feet to illuminate the subject!

It is perfectly possible to take pictures from an airplane with inexpensive cameras if the scene below is clearly defined in bright sunlight. Even better pictures can be taken with 35mm SLR cameras and, depending upon the type of film used and the brightness of the light, relatively good color and black and white pictures result. The camera in either case should be held quite close to the window glass and tilted downward or sideways to avoid reflections. At a high altitude, the shutter speed need not be faster than 1/125 of a second. But this is pointless except with the very inexpensive cameras and I recommend that speeds between 1/500 and 1/1000 be used when possible. A flashbulb can never help in an airplane; in fact, it will throw a reflection back onto the film from the window glass which will completely ruin any exposure.

But let's get back to photographing people, for this is where the flashbulb is of most use. Take care that you do not pose your subject against a mirror or a window or even a highly polished wood or chrome surface, or the light will bounce directly back into the lens of the camera. This is easy to avoid. Move your subject so that you are shooting on an angle rather than directly at the reflective surface. People wearing eyeglasses should not be photographed head on. By tilting their heads down slightly, or to the side, reflection can be avoided.

Your flash pictures at a party or at a dinner will be better if you confine yourself to medium close-ups of small groups—two, three or possibly four people—in a single scene. Move around the table, if it is a dinner, being sure that you do not have any objects obstructing your view in the foreground, and keeping the subjects five or six feet away. It is almost impossible to take an entire large dinner group without someone's eyes being closed or without the group in front being overexposed and the group in back being underexposed. About estimating the distance: many inexpensive flash cameras have a frame in the viewfinder indicating where to put your subject. Another way is to simply pace off approximately six feet.

As automation progresses in the inexpensive pocket cameras, it will soon be possible to purchase a camera that will give you as good results as you can possibly get with flash.

A continuing problem with flashbulbs is that sometimes they don't flash. The failure is usually caused by dust or grime on the base of the flashbulb where contact is made with the battery. Wipe off the base of your flashbulb before using it, and be sure that the contact points on the camera are clean. Batteries should be checked quite often, unless you are using the type of film that includes a battery in the pack.

You will get better flash pictures if the room you are photographing in is reasonably well illuminated. This is because the pupils of the eyes of your subjects will contract from the natural light around them, so that when the flash strikes the pupils they will not be noticeably red from the flash reflection. It is also much less of a shock to the subject and you're likely to get more natural expressions. Finally, remember that there are two types of flashbulbs for two kinds of film: blue for daylight, clear for tungsten. Don't mix them up.

Like flash powder and magnesium-filled bulbs, today's flashbulbs have been replaced for most professional work and most 35mm photography by electronic flash equipment. This type of light has many advantages over flashbulbs. The temperature of the light is similar to daylight, so it can be used with daylight film. It effectively stops motion, and batteries can be recharged so that the light can be used a great many times. Electronic flash has become standard lighting with news and magazine photographers, in fashion studios and, indeed, in almost all branches of professional photography. The new equipment is lightweight, and often includes a swivel flash head to make it easy to bounce the light from the ceiling. It can also be detached from the camera and moved a foot or two away. Of great importance is the fact that the light is cool rather than hot when it is discharged.

This revolutionary photographic tool was developed by Dr. Harold Edgerton at the Massachusetts Institute of Technology in Boston. His first flash equipment, though of fair intensity, was of extremely short duration. He demonstrated that even a bullet discharged from a gun could be frozen in flight. In the early forties, Edgerton photographed experimentally stopping the wings of a hummingbird in flight, a drop of milk spattering on a saucer, a golf ball pushed out of shape upon impact, with his high-speed electronic flash. Now, with much improved and yet inexpensive equipment, any amateur can duplicate most of the seemingly miraculous pictures that were done earlier in Edgerton's experiments. The extremely short duration demonstrated by him is possible today only with special equipment, for most electronic flash now has a duration of somewhere between 1/500 and 1/2000 of a second, which is enough to stop the motion of anything that you're likely to photograph. Its most important use for the amateur or semi-professional is either as a direct light source or to take incident light pictures where the illumination is bounced off a wall or ceiling.

Electronic flash is used extensively to photograph sports events. It is possible to hook up several electronic flash units (called *slave lights*) and set them off synchronized with the camera by remote control. Such lights can be controlled by radio by setting the triggering unit on a specific wavelength; when radio contact is made on that wavelength, they fire. Such radio control of cameras and electronic flash is a highly specialized field, but it is becoming more popular each day.

One more type of artificial light must be mentioned. It is a type all too often ignored, though available to every photographer. This is normal home lighting after dark—hanging lamps, floor lamps, overhead bulbs—which can be utilized for photography and give excellent results with black and white and with color tungsten film. However, results on tungsten film will be on the yellowish or warm side unless you use a compensating filter (82B or 82C) to make the flesh tones of your subject normal. Pictures with this type of existing light, especially those in color, require a tripod, a cable release and a lens shade.

A great variety of lighting effects can be arranged by moving lamps about or moving your model to where the light will be most effective. Unusual pictures can also be made with candlelight, oil lamps, gas lamps, light from a fireplace or even the light of a match.

Fluorescent light has long given amateurs and professionals problems. Pictures taken with daylight film and fluorescent light have an overall greenish tone. This can be corrected, however, by using filters known as FL-D (for daylight) and FL-B (for type B or tungsten film). They require twice as much exposure but they eliminate the green cast.

11
ACTION!

The action picture relates to many different photographic disciplines. The subject is often in motion in the documentary, the snapshot or the travel picture. But in this chapter we are discussing a specific kind of action picture, one where the subject's motion is thematized: a ballet dancer or ice skater performing, an animal running, a diver leaving the board, a child in a swing. We will also discuss another kind of action picture in which the motion is suspended but the technique of photographing the subject remains the same. This could be a tiger crouching before leaping upon its prey, racehorses lined up at the starting gate, a child about to jump into a swimming pool. The most important single thing for you to learn as a photographer is to be ready for the peak of the action or the peak of the suspended action.

How to do this? You need to condition your reflexes by learning something about the action that will take place. If you are going to photograph dancers in motion, carefully observe the dancers in rehearsal or, if that is impossible, see as many in action as you can and click off pictures you feel are pleasing to eye and mind before using film. It is amazing how rapidly one's reflexes can become conditioned. After watching performers and taking mental pictures two or three times, it becomes possible to anticipate the form that the picture will take as the dancer flows from one position to another.

Or let's consider coverage of a baseball or football game. A comprehensive knowledge of the game is essential for you to sense what type of action is going to be coming up. It is not enough to follow the action—you must anticipate it. And it is just as necessary to anticipate suspended action where the subject is not in motion. Suppose you are wandering through the zoo and suddenly come upon a bear holding a stick like a baton in the hands of an orchestra conductor. The animal is not in motion, but unless your reflexes are rapid and your camera ready, you'll miss the picture. This is often true when taking portraits: the subject will move into an interesting position, a fleeting expression (just the one you wanted) will appear, and that's the time to be ready to make the exposure. There is no substitute for eye practice, for concentrated observation of skaters, horseback riders, surfers, joggers and for leaping upon the moment that will make the picture most effective.

You must know how you want the final action picture to look. Do you want the motion frozen in midair? Do you want the action blurred to give the effect of motion? Most action photographs, especially of sports, are taken at high speed where the motion is sharply frozen. Unless you have a great deal of experience and do a considerable amount of experimentation, the use of slower shutter speeds to create a blurred figure is quite difficult, for you must be familiar with the speed of the subject as well as the speed of your shutter. A diver can be stopped in midair at 1/1000 or 1/2000 of a second. At 1/500 of a second he will be slightly blurred and at 1/250 of a second he will be blurred enough perhaps to give an interesting effect of motion. But at 1/25 of a second he will not appear on the film at all. So, unless you are entirely familiar with moving subjects and shutter speed, it is best to use a high shutter speed and stop the action wherever possible.

Even the pocket cameras, most of which have comparatively slow shutters—that is, not more than 1/250 of a second—can stop action of models and objects that move at a moderate speed. This depends, however, upon the angle of view. If the model is walking (or running slowly) directly toward you, the pocket camera can stop the motion. This would also be true of a sailboat moving either directly toward you or at a 45 degree angle. Even a leaping dancer, if caught at the top of the leap where the upward motion has reached its peak and the downward motion has not yet started, momentarily stops. At this point you don't need more than 1/250 of a second, and sometimes even 1/100 of a second is enough to produce a sharp action photograph. But remember, if you are using a pocket or Polaroid camera, you are unlikely to have a fast enough shutter to stop action which moves across your line of vision.

Another effective action technique is *panning* or moving the camera along at the same speed as the moving model. This means that if an animal is running across your line of vision, you can follow it, keeping it in your viewfinder and pressing the shutter as you continue to move at the same speed as the animal. Even with a comparatively slow shutter of 1/100 or 1/250 of a second, it is possible to stop the action but blur the background. This is extremely effective, especially in color photographs. The animal seems to be running at a relatively high speed even though it may not be. This effect is produced, of course, by the blurring of the background. It is a good technique for you to use for moving vehicles, trains, runners and, in fact, any person or object moving across the camera's range.

Now you have observed your dancers, surfers, baseball players, etc., and you have determined in what direction the action is likely to move. But how can you be sure to have your camera ready? Here the automatic camera can be a great help. To focus, you may either estimate the distance from the camera to the point where the action is going to take place, and focus on that spot, or set the scale at the number of feet estimated from camera to subject. Exposure adjustments will depend upon what type of automatic you have. If it is the type where you set the lens opening and the photocell sets the speed, then it will be necessary for you to use a relatively large opening so that the camera can function at a high shutter speed. If your automatic selects the lens opening, then it is best for you to set the shutter speed at 1/1000 or 1/2000 of a second and let the photocell adjust. Then follow the action until it reaches the spot where you have prefocused and press the shutter button. Prefocusing should be practiced by anyone interested in sports photography, because to get the picture sharp and clear the camera must be focused on the action spot. And, if your camera does not have automatic exposure, it is imperative to set the exposure in advance and to continually reset it as the light changes.

Let's take the five types of cameras we discussed in Chapter 2 and see how each of them adapts to action pictures. Far and away the most useful and the most used by professional sports and animal photographers is the automated or semi-automated SLR 35mm camera. I have discussed many of its qualities in the chapter on SELECTING YOUR CAMERA but there are a number of additional advantages that these cameras have for action photography. The greatest advantage is a motor, which can be attached to the more expensive type of SLR. Motors add to the weight of the camera but they allow for short bursts of exposures close together and without the necessity of your advancing the film.

The motor has three important functions: it advances the film automatically, it cocks the shutter and, when you hold the release button down, exposures become continuous. Motors can be set for single exposures or an entire roll of film can be run off in seven seconds. This makes the motor drive valuable for certain types of sequences involving time-lapse photography, animals or continuous sports action.

The serious amateur who wants to do time-lapse photography—showing the opening of a flower over a number of hours, for instance—could find the motor quite useful, especially when it is set up with a self-timing system so that exposures are made by the clock and the motor rather than by the photographer.

Professional sports photographers find the motorized SLR almost indispensable. To get the sequence showing the winning horse coming from behind at a race requires a more rapid burst of exposure than the photographer could possibly make manually. A sequence showing a hurdler taking off, in midair and landing requires a motorized camera.

The motorized camera can also be used with remote control. This is important in photographing birds and animals when the presence of the photographer would be disturbing. It also allows the photographer to be in two, or even three, places at the same time. For instance, at a horse race, he can set up two radio-controlled cameras in different spots and operate another one manually, thus photographing the race from three different angles simultaneously. I once had an SLR camera built into the costume of an ice skater. Then, seated in the audience with my radio control, I was able to take pictures as though I were skating around the ice during the performance. The possibilities for the remote control camera are only beginning to be explored, but so far they are not for anyone except the very advanced amateur or the professional.

The disadvantages of the motor drive for the amateur include, first, the cost, which is usually more than that of the camera itself; second, a tendency to shoot many more frames than one needs, which increases film cost; and, third, the additional weight and noise, both of which make the camera more conspicuous and less likely to be used in a "candid" way. The motors are detachable, but it is all too easy to get used to one and to wind up shooting hundreds of unnecessary pictures.

Still another advantage of the 35mm SLR is the fact that the more expensive ones have shutter speeds going up to 1/2000 of a second. This brief shutter opening will stop the motion of any animal traveling at any speed or the motion in any sporting event.

Generally speaking, the 35mm rangefinder cameras, because they are in a lower price bracket (except for the Leica), do not have motor drives available. Yet many of them have shutter speeds of 1/1000 of a second and can be used for action photography. In fact, most action, as I have previously pointed out, can be stopped at 1/500 of a second, and some action at 1/250 of a second. But the rangefinder camera can be a little slower when it comes to focusing. And, on models where the rangefinder and the viewfinder are separate, so that the eye has to focus and then move to the viewer, it becomes almost impossible to photograph the peak action.

The speeds of most pocket cameras are not really fast enough for close-up action. Many of them will stop relatively slow-moving action at a distance. All of them can be used to follow the action and photograph the action while the camera and the subject are moving at the same speed, as I have described above. You can take home an overall shot of the football game or of your girlfriend or boyfriend cheering, but don't expect to get a great close-up of a pass being intercepted or a wild drive for a touchdown. This kind of picture requires an SLR with a telephoto lens and a high-speed shutter.

The instant picture cameras suffer from the same problems as the rangefinder cameras. They are not equipped with high-speed shutters. Rangefinding and viewfinding, except for the XL-70, is either fixed-focus or requires looking through the rangefinder, then the viewfinder. This slows things down too much for sports or animal photography.

The 2¼ by 2¼ single lens reflex cameras are another matter entirely. Shutter speeds are fast enough. Focusing is through the lens and rapid. Motors are available. Many photographers, especially in the commercial, fashion and architectural fields, like these cameras because they give a large negative or transparency. This makes for enlargements with less grain and, depending upon the film and processing, more detail. The difference, however, between 35mm and 2¼ by 2¼ in transparencies and prints for the amateur is not great enough, in my opinion, to make up for the larger format.

The 2¼ by 2¼ has several drawbacks. Its size and weight is one; cost is another. Not only is the cost of the camera itself astronomical, but film and print expenses are also high. Furthermore, though it has an eye level adjustment, it is basically constructed for chest level viewing. This creates a major problem in action pictures, for you cannot view with two eyes open looking out at the action as you can with the SLR; you must wait until the action moves into the reflex finder. But if you do so, it is likely to have passed the reflex finder before you can press the button. The problem is alleviated by the fact that this type of camera is now obtainable with prism finders, which do function at eye level.

One of the most satisfying areas of exploration for the amateur photographer is collecting animal pictures. Animals can be photographed with any of the cameras discussed, although the best pictures have been taken with a camera that has at least a medium telephoto lens. But remember, it is not the camera that takes good pictures of animals, or anything else, it is the photographer. Again, observation is the key and patience is an absolute essential for taking good animal pictures.

Just as effective animal studies can be done in the zoo, and especially in the wild animal parks that have sprung up all over the world, as in the wild. In most zoos you can find an animal family—giraffes with their young, or bears or kangaroos—and observation of family relationships pays off in good pictures. It is even possible to do portraits of animals (you will need a 200mm lens or zoom lens for this). Suppose you are photographing a gorilla behind bars. By focusing on the animal itself, it is sometimes possible to render the bars so out of focus as to make them scarcely noticeable. Fortunately, most zoos no longer have their animals behind bars but behind moats, which make them better subjects.

My advice is to take a lightweight folding chair and a light tripod, measure the exposure, or let your automated camera do it, focus on the zone where the animal is or where you expect it to be, and then wait. Sooner or later the animal will greet another animal that arrives, or scratch its chin with its hind leg, or begin to browse for grass, lie down, turn around or, if you are lucky, get into a picture pose that interests you. Then, click goes the shutter. I would recommend that a preliminary hour be spent observing even before taking any pictures, for animals have a pattern of movement and, when they are used to your presence, they go through their normal routine without noticing you. Some animals are more shy than others. That is something you will learn from observation.

Photographing wild animals in their natural habitat requires a different approach.The photographer must move slowly and quietly, and not approach too closely. It is usually best, in those areas where animals have become used to jeeps—such as the great wild animal preserves of East and South Africa—to travel by jeep, for the animals pay little attention to the vehicle's occupants. It is possible to get within a few yards of lions, giraffes and rhinos when they are browsing. But movements should be deliberately slow, and clothing as inconspicuous as possible. Water holes are among the best places in the early morning to photograph animals and birds. They are so intent upon going about their routine that they pay little attention to photographers, unless the photographer gets too close or is wearing a white or red shirt or has a particularly noisy camera.

Professional animal photographers study the habits of wild animals well enough to know where to find them, how closely they can be approached safely, what time of day is best for stalking them. Generally speaking—and this goes for zoos as well as in the wild—dawn to 9 AM and 4 to 7 PM are the best times to find animals available and alert. In the heat of the day most animals get into as cool a spot as possible, lie down and stay there. So you have to get up early in the morning or be out late in the afternoon for the percentages to be with you.

The same general rules apply to the photography of pets. Many people have pets for many years and never observe their habits, or their unique characteristics. So start out with observation. Then, when you're ready to photograph, stalk your pet carefully in the same way you would a wild animal. Do not make sudden movements to frighten it away. And if you must place it in a background that you feel will make a more interesting picture, move it there, then move away. But have the camera prefocused and ready so that as soon as you move away you can make the exposures. As in all action pictures, anticipating the subject's probable movement and having your camera ready to record the exact moment you want are imperative.

It is worthwhile to consider using a theme around which to build a file of animal transparencies or prints. Such a theme might be "mothers with their young" or even "young animals." Most zoos have a nursery section where young animals can be photographed, sometimes with, sometimes without, their mothers. You might try a sequence as though you were going to do a short book about your cat or dog. Consider observing the animal for a day and then building a sequence out of its movements. Or try a series at the zoo with close-ups of different animals eating. There are literally hundreds of ways to build an interesting sequence of animal pictures. But whichever one you choose, you will find that observation and preparation are essential.

To a great many photographers the most important field for action pictures is the photography of children. It is also one of the most difficult. But it need not be. First you must realize that there are two kinds of children: the kind that follow you around trying to get you to take their picture and the kind that absolutely refuse to allow it. There is a danger that even the ones that follow you around asking you to take their picture will change and hate the whole idea. There is nothing mysterious about their negative attitude: it is based on the kind of treatment they usually get from their photographing elders.

They are told to hold still—and what child wants to hold still? They are told to shut up and stop talking when they are having their pictures taken. They are not allowed to frown, and they are not supposed to squint even when the sun is shining directly into their eyes. If you enforce this sort of behavior when photographing children, and I am inclined to think most people do, you have lost them, perhaps permanently, as models. No adult would stand for the kind of photographic treatment kids are expected to endure.

So, what to do? Well, let's start out by treating the children at least as well as we would animals. Let's not expect them to keep still. Let's keep their eyes out of the sun. And, if they want to frown, let them frown. By taking your pictures of children when they are unaware, you're likely to get their most interesting gestures and expressions. If you are going to photograph children and expect cooperation, let them in on the game. Explain the camera and what you are trying to achieve in the photograph. Make them a part of your effort. Take your pictures of children in shaded areas where they won't have to squint. You wouldn't tell an adult to smile for a portrait; you'd be more inclined to tell an amusing story—so try a story on the children.

Small babies are easy to photograph if you put them in soft light, prop them up at a good compositional angle, then start smiling or waving a bright object to attract their attention. It is sometimes even better to use the patient observation technique. Spend a half hour or so with the baby on the floor, letting it move as it will, and photographing when you think the photograph is likely to be expressive. The same rules go for making color transparencies as for making color or black and white prints. Avoid sunlight except as backlighting and, if you want to show the modeling and the contour of the child's face as well as a natural expression, avoid flashbulbs. If you must use some flash, electronic flash is best. It is easier on the eyes and the light winks so quickly that the child is hardly aware of it. Electronic flash also stops any motion, which is not true of flashbulbs.

It is best not to dress up babies or children to have their pictures taken. If they are old enough, let them select their own outfit; it will be more expressive of their own personality than the way you dress them. Above all, don't make a big, dramatic, world-shaking event out of photographing your children or anyone else's, and don't lose your temper. Remember, photography is supposed to be a pleasurable experience for you and the children as well. Because children are, by nature, lively, let your pictures reflect it. Photograph them in action whenever possible. Even a portrait can have spontaneity.

Choreographer showing use of dance notation handbook. Triple exposure on a single 35mm film with automatic SLR which allows multiple exposures by pressing rewind button without advancing film. Lights were electronic flash.

With the camera prefocused and set at 1/1000 of a second, it was easy to catch actor Sean Connery with both feet off the ground. Few photographers use all the potentials in time, speed and depth that are available on most cameras.

No sun, overcast sky and a softball game. Here the action was stopped with a 1/125 of a second just as the pitcher reached to catch ball. Don't hesitate to try to stop action like this even with inexpensive pocket cameras.

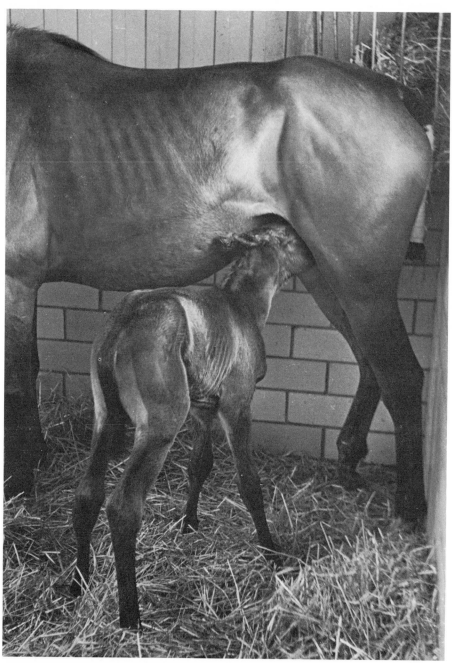

A newborn foal stands up to nurse for the first time. This kind of action shot requires careful preparation. I waited most of night with flash ready, camera focused and mounted on light tripod, then shot in natural light at sunup.

A suspended action picture. The curious giraffe was not even in the picture that I planned to take of the young hippos. As I saw it approach and lean over, I quickly backed away, rechecked the viewfinder and then refocused.

With concentration and control, the controversial author and, incidentally, table-tennis buff, Henry Miller, delivers his fast ball to make the point. Light was from two floodlights in reflectors bounced off the ceiling. Shutter speed was 1/250 of a second.

A 25-pound salmon leaps upstream. An action picture that took patience, preparation, good reflexes and luck. With fast film, shutter set at 1/1000, lens at f/11, I waited half an hour. When this big one jumped, I was ready.

International champion ice skater Ronnie Robertson leaps over women's skating champion Cathy Machado in this multiple electronic flash sequence shot on one negative. Miss Machado glided across the ice while Robertson jumped just be-

hind her and above her. Four electronic units were used, the camera shutter was open for 1/2 second and a 4-contact switch controlled by the photographer activated each of the four flashes in sequence. Picture was made for Ice Capades.

Rock singer Estelle Weir of the Weir family band was deep into her song. I used a number one fog filter for atmosphere, opened up the lens to blur the background and waited for her to hold a high note. Exposure was made outdoors on a rainy day.

Patience around animals always pays off. Sooner or later they will move and the movement is sometimes interesting, though the wait can seem interminable. Shot with a zoom lens at about 80mm after spending the morning waiting.

The action was fast and fierce as these very young karate students performed in New York's Central Park. I stood on the edge of the audience waiting for the kick, the concentration and reaction. Exposure at 1/500 of a second.

By waiting for the right moment, this picture could be taken with almost any camera. Necessary ingredients are brave child, lots of pigeons (there are always plenty in St. Mark's Square, Venice), patience and a steady shutter finger.

I planned to shoot leopards feeding and arranged to go out in my car while the keeper took the food in his jeep. I took this unique picture as the hungry leopards leaped on the jeep trying to reach the keeper and their breakfast.

The story was called "Every Dog Should Have a Man," and I photographed writer Corey Ford at his Maine home with his constant companion. It was a cloudy, rainy day, 1/125 of a second at f/2.8 on fast film—not enough to completely stop the motion.

Blurred motion in this rape scene from the motion picture "HUD" (Paul Newman and Patricia Neal) was achieved by slow shutter speed of 1/5 of a second. This type of slowed action is most effective to visualize motion.

12
A SHORT HISTORY OF PHOTOGRAPHY

The ancestor of the modern camera was created about 70 years after Columbus discovered the New World. In those fertile, adventurous, imaginative days of the Italian Renaissance the properties of a magic box were first explored. In the year 1558 Giovanni Battista della Porta exposed the information that he had gathered about the *camera obscura*, which can be translated as "dark room." The history of the camera is the history of a large dark room with a tiny hole in it that, like Alice in Wonderland, diminished in size until it could be carried about in a small pocket.

Leonardo da Vinci, artist, inventor, poet, described in one of his monographs the manner in which the *camera obscura* operated. He, like other Renaissance artists, while seeking ways to understand and reproduce scenes in perspective, learned that a room completely dark with a hole in one wall accurately projected the scene *upside down* on the opposite wall of the room. We may surmise that some of these early Renaissance artists tried standing on their heads to do their sketching, judging by the results. They probably would have been better off continuing to work from nature, but science and laziness got the better of them. Yet we should be grateful to these "dark room" pioneers, for without them the invention of the little black box we call a camera would certainly have been delayed.

During the following decade the scientist-artists made a great breakthrough. By 1570, it was discovered that by putting a piece of convex glass (shaped like the lens of the eye) into the peephole one could make the image clearer by moving the canvas or paper forward or back. The scene came into sharp focus. Soon industrious artists were mounting canvases on a frame with wheels so that within the confines of the dark room copies of the reflected scene could be easily made and the varied colors of nature easily filled in.

The camera really began to shrink when some ingenious pictorialist figured out a way to make the dark room portable. He put the lens in one end of the box and at the other end placed a square of ground glass. By putting a black cloth over his head, he could then take this box about, point it at any lighted object and make an accurate tracing on the glass. This short cut to accurate perspective and color became a device that few artists could resist, especially after a mirror, placed at a 45° angle, was mounted inside the box and the ground glass put on top rather than on the back of the camera. Artists no longer had to stand on their heads; copying was no longer a pain in the neck, for the mirror turned the image *right side up* and artists could make accurate tracings by laying a transparent paper or thin cloth over the glass. But, mind you, this did not happen all at once. It took 200 years of box making, lens placing and experimentation with mirrors before the magic box was portable and practical.

Before a true camera, as we know it, was invented, a most difficult scientific development had to take place. For although a camera is only a black box with a lens and a mirror, it was essential, if the reflected image was to be *preserved,* that a material upon which light could be permanently recorded replace the ground glass. The problem was to trap the elusive image. If this could be accomplished, the artist would not have to trace it by hand; the camera alone could record the scene permanently. Even duplication might become possible.

Alchemists, chemists, artists and magicians had dabbled for hundreds of years with the effects of light in nature. Light shining on certain plants was known to change the plant's color. Dyes, when put into fabrics and left in the sun, changed color. But it took a German physicist who experimented with silver salts, Johann Heinrich Schulze, and a well-shaken cocktail of nitric acid, silver and chalk to solve, or dissolve, the problem. The effect of bright sunlight on his decanter turned the mixture purple. Other scientists turned green but Schulze had discovered that the light of the sun, rather than its heat, could change the color of silver salts. This may not sound like too much of a discovery today, but it was the clue leading to the coating of film. This gave two Frenchmen the information that led to the successful making of a primitive type of film capable of holding onto the image reflected by the lens.

Americans, Germans and especially Japanese find it difficult to pronounce one of these Frenchmen's names. It was Niépce (which is pronounced "nyeps") who deserves the credit. Joseph Nicéphore Niépce had a lot of help from another Frenchman with a slightly less difficult name and one which became a byword in Europe and America. This was Louis Jacques Mandé Daguerre. Without him we would not have the daguerreotype of your grandmother or grandfather with their silvery brown tones. Nor would the antique dealers and photography museums and galleries be able to reflect the age of Daguerre and Niépce, the late 1830s, forties and fifties and to charge outrageous prices for your grim and severe looking ancestral portraits.

The popularity of the daguerreotype is amusingly illustrated by the following story. A ragged beggar approached a well-dressed man in the financial district of Paris. He told the affluent gentleman that his wife and children were hungry and that he needed a few francs to buy food. The rich man reluctantly gave him the money and each went on their way. But the next day, at the same spot, the same man approached his benefactor of the day before with exactly the same story about his starving wife and children. "But," said the rich man, "what happened to the money I gave you yesterday?" "Well," said the beggar, "as I approached my house, I held up the money for my wife and children to see, as they were standing at the gate. As I came closer and closer, I saw the smiles on their faces. They looked so beautiful that I took them right out and had their pictures taken."

Factual or not, the story is true in spirit, for there were few homes on any economic level that did not have a picture of maman or papa or bébé or grand-père or grand-mère—and this craze to record the image of loved ones for posterity quickly spread all over the world.

In these early days there was a great deal of suffering attached to being photographed in the studios that sprang up in cities and villages. The sensitized daguerreotype surface was so insensitive that it was necessary to have concentrated brilliant light on the subject. It was also necessary to keep the subject still, which is why the first great photographers Niépce and Daguerre, as well as William Henry Fox Talbot in England, Samuel F. B. Morse, the American, and other patient portraitists became exasperated working with even the most patient models. Some of the exposures took as much as 10 to 20 minutes with the sun either directly upon or reflected onto the face of the sitter by mirrors. Some of the weeping and wailing and gnashing of teeth is reflected in the expressions of the sitters.

Although daguerreotype film became somewhat more sensitive and lenses gathered more light to make exposures shorter, the daguerreotype had an additional drawback. Each one was one of a kind. There was no negative and no way to make duplicates. The move away from the daguerreotype to a kind of photograph that could be reproduced many times came from an English astronomer who gets little space in most histories of photography. Sir John Herschel, at a time when Daguerre's process and that of the English scientist Fox Talbot were both being held as close secrets, noted that three essentials would be necessary to produce a good picture: a very susceptible paper, a very perfect camera and a means of arresting or stopping the action of the light effect upon the silver salts. He found that he could wash away from the sensitized paper the chloride of silver with a solution of hyposulphite of soda which fixed the image. The same process is used today, although sodium thiosulfate is used instead of the hyposulphite of 130 years ago. Yet photographers still call the solution used as a "fixing bath" *hypo*.

It was Herschel who named the reverse image *negative* and suggested that a *positive* could be made. Fox Talbot got all the credit for this because Herschel was not really very interested in pursuing the process and allowed Fox Talbot to report it. It was this breakthrough that made multiple prints possible from a single negative—by making the negative itself permanent.

The history of amateurs in photography and their importance begins toward the end of the 19th century after the invention of the permanent negative. Not only artists but businessmen, writers and salesmen began producing historically memorable pictures. And by 1900 the amateur was taking many more pictures than the professional. Most of these were snapshots. Yet the serious amateur made an important contribution to photographic history.

Perhaps the best known of the amateurs was Lewis Carroll, author of *Alice in Wonderland,* who made many thoughtful and even a few unposed pictures of little girls including Alice Liddell, who was the original Alice in Wonderland. Oliver Wendell Holmes, poet and jurist, made some excellent photographs. But perhaps the most effective of the amateurs was a woman, Julia Margaret Cameron, who produced a series of portraits that for style and dignity have rarely, if ever, been surpassed. Among others, she photographed such outstanding men of her time as Henry Wadsworth Longfellow, Charles Darwin, Robert Browning, and Alfred, Lord Tennyson to mention only a few.

These were amateurs in the noblest sense. They sensitized their own plates, did their own development and risked hand burns from the caustic processing solutions. There is a small but visually important volume in print called *Victorian Children* which includes effective pictures by both amateurs and professionals of the period between 1850 and 1860. It vividly displays the poor, ill-treated children of the Victorian era including child prostitutes ranging in age from 10 to 14.

Inventions have always thrived on warfare. Photography developed rapidly during the Crimean War, and the rebellions in India against the British. The American Civil War was covered photographically more thoroughly than any previous conflict. Mathew Brady, photographer and entrepreneur, gathered around him a great team and proceeded to record just about everything that would stand still long enough for his still clumsy cameras and insensitive negative material. Because there was no danger of their moving, the Brady team photographed a hundred dead men to each live one, and the negatives are littered with dead horses, overturned cannon and battlefields strewn with corpses. It is no wonder that, following this debacle visualized in static images, the next step was to get some life and action into the photographic scene.

The photographer who accomplished this, and in a memorable way, was Edward James Muggeridge (who had his name changed to Eadweard Muybridge, a dubious improvement). Muggeridge, or Muybridge, a volatile, passionate man by nature (he killed his wife's lover in a moment of stress) contended that, contrary to the prevailing opinion of contemporary artists, running horses *did* manage to get all four feet off the ground at the same time. He proved his point, and in the process developed an improved camera. He developed a fast shutter which he claimed to be faster than a 1/1000 of a second. He fitted 12 cameras with these shutters, then stretched release strings across a track which a horse, as it galloped past, broke. The resulting action silhouettes (he had stretched white canvas across the back of the track) clearly showed that all four feet of the horse did leave the ground at one time. It proved that the camera was quicker than the eye—that the artists who had been drawing horses had never been able to observe them accurately. By making a strip of his pictures and passing them before a slit in a piece of paper, the effect of the horse actually moving was achieved and in this way Muybridge's work can be considered as part of the development of the motion picture.

Muybridge went on to do a series of studies of completely nude athletes against a background of lined paper so that each part of the motion could be studied. He greatly shocked both the scientific and publishing worlds when his 11 volumes of photographs called *Animal Locomotion* appeared. He had not only photographed animals of all kinds but he had used his human male and female models entirely nude and had shown them in every possible situation he could devise, such as a nude girl sweeping the floor, throwing a bucket of water on another; men, their genitalia bouncing, were shown jumping, fencing and wrestling. Muybridge's pictures are still among the great action pictures of all time. Although he intended to create a book for the use of artists, his work extended to scientific circles and became a landmark in the history of photography. The book has been reprinted many times and, although the first edition appeared in 1887, it is still in print.

But photography was still in the hands of professionals, scientists and artists and remained there until an American minister with the unlikely name of Hannibal Goodwin patented a transparent roll film in 1887 which could be put into the black box so that anyone could take a picture. At about the same time George Eastman patented a small box camera which he called a Kodak, because the word *kodak* sounded to him like the clicking of the shutter. To me, it always sounded like *tick* or *tock*. At any rate, with the small black box containing a piece of convex glass on one end and film in the other it became possible for everyone to take a picture. The snapshot was born.

The voyeur aspect of the camera and the opportunity to spy with it began to be explored about the time that Eastman released his Kodak. Other cameras appeared on the market in disguise. Some were made in the form of handbags or suitcases. Others were made to look like books, and many were actually used as "detective" cameras to gather evidence to be used later in court. But it was the general public that responded to the new, easy to use, cameras. Eastman sold his first camera for about $25, complete with enough film to take a hundred negatives. The price of the camera included the price of the film, and the camera had to be sent back to the factory for the film to be processed and prints made. You got your prints back, with the camera reloaded for another hundred shots, for the price of $10. This started the Eastman program of making foolproof cameras. Their slogan was "You press the button, we do the rest." It was the beginning of a system that Eastman, with its modern, ever smaller camera, still follows today. Eastman's program includes a series of automatic cameras that take pre-packaged films that can be taken out of the camera and returned to Eastman; they still do the rest, sending you back your finished prints as color positives, transparencies or black and white prints just as George Eastman promised. The cost, of course, has greatly increased, but so has the quality of the pictures.

But we're getting ahead of ourselves. Photography started out as an aid to artists; it developed into a technique for recording immobile objects; it became a semi-scientific tool in the exploration of motion and then it slowly began to go back to the artists again. Salons, supported by both professionals and amateurs, sprang up in Europe and America. Photo clubs, which sometimes included artists in their membership, proliferated. Out of these international exhibitions and activities the work of a number of men and women photographers emerged, the best known of which was Alfred Stieglitz, an American of German descent who began winning international prizes as early as 1891. Stieglitz produced all kinds of pictures—extraordinary portraits (it was said that with a hidden camera he once photographed the face of a woman in sexual orgasm), documentary pictures such as horses drawing streetcars through the icy New York streets, still lifes and pictures in which action was just sufficiently stopped to be most effective. His influence on the camera world was electrifying. He used both large and small cameras.

One of the great moments in photography, and a moment that opened the modern school of photography, was Stieglitz' Photo-Secession exhibition at the National Arts Club in 1902. Two of the founders of the group that arranged the Photo-Secession exhibition exerted for the next 60 years great personal influence on photography in the world. They were the late Edward Steichen and Clarence H. White. They published a magazine called *Camera Work* which still exists. It was the teaching and writing of Clarence White and the exciting quality of the photographs made by both White and Steichen that won photography its first recognition as a truly important new art form. In Stieglitz' Little Galleries, an outgrowth of the Photo-Secession movement, art and photography were displayed on an equal level. Stieglitz brought artists' work from Europe that had never been seen by Americans before, such as that of Rodin, Cézanne, Matisse and Picasso, and introduced the Americans Dove, Weber and Marin—and the outstanding woman painter, Georgia O'Keeffe. Hanging next to the paintings of these young masters were the photographs of Stieglitz, Steichen and White.

With the work of these pioneers it was as though the peephole which had let a limited amount of light into the dark room had become a huge window looking out upon the world. They had combined the eye of the camera with the eye of the perceptive, sensitive photographer. A new art form was born. Their work inspired and opened up the paths to be explored by Paul Strand, Charles Sheeler and Edward Weston.

The paths led in many directions. Edward Steichen, a man of tremendous energy, taste and talent, for many years specialized in portraits and fashion photography, as magazines like *Vogue* and *Harper's Bazaar* became leaders in avant-garde photography. Edward Weston worked with a large 8 x 10" camera and founded the f/64 (smallest possible aperture) school. These men replaced the romantics who worked with soft focus lenses to create sentimental genre scenes and landscapes. The difference was electrifying. The stage was being effectively set for the advent of modern photography.

This came with the beginning of the Roosevelt era. The new radical structure of the United States Department of Agriculture included the employment of one of the true pioneers in the development of photography. He was Roy Stryker, a visionary, an idealist and a helluva organizer. He gathered around him a group of men and women to document the latter days of the depression. The photographers that included Dorothea Lange, Walker Evans, Ben Shahn, Carl Mydans, Arthur Rothstein, Russell Lee, John Vachon, Marion Post Wolcott, John Collier and Gordon Parks photographed a compassionate visual history of the thirties. They photographed the topsoil of the dust bowl of Oklahoma literally blowing away, the black sharecroppers evicted from absentee owned farms, the plight of the migratory workers, boredom on the assembly line, starvation in the cotton fields. They produced 270,000 pictures for Stryker's Farm Security Administration. Their pictures had such impact that they helped to change life in the USA by focusing public attention on the desperate condition of the group that President Roosevelt called "one-third of a nation." This now priceless collection of documentary photographs reposes in the Library of Congress.

It was while these dedicated and concerned photographers were revealing the human condition in the USA that the modern picture magazine was born. There had been attempts, beginning with *Mid-Week Pictorial* as early as 1914, to found a picture magazine. The *National Geographic* contributed to its development, but it was not until *Life* and *Look* were founded in 1936 that the actual picture magazine appeared. *Life's* written credo read:

"To see life, to see the world; to eyewitness great events; to watch the faces of the poor and the gestures of the proud; to see strange things—machines, armies, multitudes, shadows in the jungle and on the moon; to see man's work—his paintings, towers, and discoveries;

to see things a thousand miles away, things hidden behind walls and within rooms, things dangerous to come to; the women that men love and many children; to see and to take pleasure in seeing; to see and be amazed; to see and be instructed."

From its beginning *Life* employed the great photographers of the world. Indeed, photographers became the aristocracy of the magazine, for its publishers realized that it was their pictures that sold the magazine to its millions of subscribers. Its editors took the position that the picture came first—before the word. *Life* kept the promise of its credo and two weeks after it appeared *Look* magazine was published. It, too, featured excellent photographs and great photographers but it did not reflect the news directly. It was a feature magazine rather than a news magazine. Yet its appeal was, like *Life's*, largely visual. The photographers of both *Life* and *Look* produced an exhilarating, thoughtful, shocking, intimate view of the world. They showed life and death, blood and guts, tenderness, sorrow, joy, sex and love as the photographers, each with his or her own skill and camera gear, went forth to record moments big and small in the lives of men and women.

The stars in the photographic galaxy were by no means all men. Margaret Bourke-White, a beauty with an unerring instinct to be in the right place at the right time, photographed *Life's* first lead story and its first cover in Fort Peck, Montana. She and her camera were on hand for some of the most explosive events of World War II in Purple Heart Valley and with Patton in France and Germany. Her expressive coverage ranged from harrowing famine scenes in India (and Gandhi's agonizing struggle for India's independence) to the blacks in the underground diamond mines of South Africa. She was with the guerrilla army in Korea. Indeed, from her early documentary photographic coverage made into a book called *You Have Seen Their Faces*, which dealt with the sharecroppers of the South, to her final work in the mid-sixties, she photographed the climax of critical events of the world.

Other great women photojournalists included Nina Leen, whose essays appeared in *Life* and the fashion magazines and in books spanning a period of 30 years, and Lisa Larson, whose specialty was photographing international celebrities and tracing socially significant trends.

Even before women began risking their lives, a cigar-smoking, poker-playing Hungarian American had begun his career by photographing the civil war in Spain in 1936. His name was Robert Capa. He continued to cover one war after another until he was killed by a land mine in Indochina in 1954. W. Eugene Smith was wounded in World War II but went on to become one of the great photo essayists of his time. David Douglas Duncan revealed the life of the foot soldier in the Korean War; he became not only an outstanding photojournalist, but author and illustrator of his own books as well. Larry Burrows showed war in Viet Nam day by day as it was being fought, and was shot down in a helicopter as he continued to photograph during the last days of the conflict. Dicky Chapelle, a fine woman photojournalist, also died in that war. It must be remembered that these men and women and other photojournalists produced memorable photographs and picture essays on subjects which were far removed from the world at war.

Between 1936 and 1970 *Life, Look, Time, Newsweek,* London's *Picture Post,* France's *Paris Match, Vogue, Harper's Bazaar, the Saturday Evening Post* and *Holiday* found themselves becoming increasingly dependent upon the free-lance fraternity of photographers in addition to their staffs. A whole new breed of photographers emerged—men and women willing to experiment, to take risks, to travel over the world, to give voice to photography as a universal language.

Gjon Mili experimented successfully to make stroboscopic light a popular photographic tool. Henri Cartier-Bresson exposed his film candidly at "the decisive moment." Irving Penn created images with taste and sensitivity. Ernst Haas immigrated from Europe to become one of the great color specialists in the USA. Philippe Halsman produced over 100 *Life* magazine covers. Best known of all *Life* photographers was Alfred Eisenstaedt, whose outstanding portraits, news coverage and photographic essays appeared over the entire span of *Life's* existence—more than 35 years. Ansel Adams photographed the grandeur of the West. Richard Avedon exposed in light and shadow the beauty and the ugliness of the rich and famous. Arnold Newman made portraits of world figures that reflected their environment. They were a small group but they helped to make photography universally acceptable.

To do their work they needed small, dependable, high-speed cameras and the photographic industry responded with many of the cameras, meters and lights that are now part of the new photography.

When death, as it must to all magazines, came to *Life,* its photographers and other photographers imbued with the same spirit continued to take great pictures of the human family. Out of the picture magazine era came one of the great contributing factors in the development of modern photojournalism. This was the organization in 1945 of the American Society of Magazine Photographers, a small group of free-lance photojournalists interested in maintaining their integrity as photographers and expanding their earnings. It grew slowly at first and in recent years more rapidly to become the Society of Photographers in Communications, an organization of over 1200 photographers that sets standards of excellence for its members, keeps a wary eye on unethical practices by publishers and advertisers (and by photographers as well) and has helped to set the high standards that editorial and advertising photography has achieved. Its membership numbers the most noted photographers in the world.

A new chapter in photographic history is being written, perhaps the most important chapter in many years. For the first time original prints by recent photographers, some still living, are bringing prices that compare with those of etchings, lithographs and even paintings. An Alfred Stieglitz print recently brought a price of $4,500. Prints by living photographers as well as vintage prints are sought after by museums and collectors. A whole new profession, curator of photographic prints, has developed in major museums. Even major art galleries are giving shows to photographers. One of the most notable of these was the retrospective show of Richard Avedon's work at the prestigious Marlboro Gallery in the fall of 1975. Thousands of people attended, and more of them came to look at the Avedon pictures than at the paintings of Picasso and Matisse exhibited in a nearby gallery. At least 3,000 people found their way to the exhibition. This was by no means the first time photography had been exhibited as art by a reputable gallery, but it was the first super show where the photographer's work was given commercial recognition as a fine art.

Photographic records from the past, daguerreotypes, negatives from the glass negative era, sepia tone prints from the early 1900's have become collectors' items. There is a mad scramble on to buy up great photographic works of the past and of the present. Alongside the art galleries, photographic galleries have sprung up throughout the world. From them the public is buying photographs to hang on their walls and to treasure as investments, just as earlier generations bought lithographs, etchings and drawings. Visually oriented books sell by the hundreds of thousands. Each year a larger proportion of visual books is published. Indeed, there is a special publishing world that exists by producing and distributing the picture book.

Photographic schools are turning out potentially fine photographers in large numbers. Free-lancers are experimenting in many different directions. Camera clubs, made up of amateur and semi-professional members, continually add new dimensions to the visual image. Advertising and fashion photography has continued techniques from the past and invented new ones. The work of photojournalists is seen in publications from Italy to Iran, from the U.S. to the USSR. New types of equipment, manual, semi-automated and automated, give a creative outlet to millions of people. These men and women who have made photography a part of their lives, the amateurs, semi-professionals and the professionals, will produce the visual history of tomorrow. The photographs being made today will become the great and much sought after prints of the future.

ACKNOWLEDGEMENTS

I have been very fortunate in having as colleagues and friends many distinguished photographers, technicians and art directors who contributed to my success as a photographer. Among them were Charles Tudor, *Life Magazine's* late great art director, and Dave Stech who worked with him. From them I learned about cropping, editing and simplicity of presentation. I was also fortunate enough to work for *Life* while Ed Thompson was picture editor and then long-time editor. Others who contributed to my photographic education were Wilson Hicks, who gave me my first assignment, Maitland Edey, who encouraged me to experiment, and Phil Kunhardt Jr., whose door was always open for advice and counsel. I remember learning a great deal from the first important book on photojournalism, *Photography Is a Language*, and from its author, my friend John Whiting, and from columnist-author John Adam Knight.

My mentors in the field of black and white printing were Manya Sweet, Ralph Baum and Harry Amdur. Early lessons in the use and misuse of color came from Paul Outerbridge. For my first action color cover photographed for *Life*, I had the personal assistance of the developer of the strobe, or speedlight, Dr. Harold Edgerton of M.I.T., in 1946. We set up experimental lights at the Boston Garden where Ice Capades was playing. While on the subject of technical help, my various and ever-changing cameras have been kept in perfect condition by three outstanding camera technicians, O. G. Heinemann, Marty Forsher and Al Schneider.

I owe a debt to many photographer friends. No photographic question has ever been too difficult for David Eisendrath, dean of technical photographers, to answer—and he has always had time. But then, all my photographer friends have given me of their time and knowledge. Eliot Elisofon, while preparing gourmet dinners; Jerry Cooke at the Kentucky Derby, the Tokyo and Mexico Olympics; Margaret Bourke-White, as we danced our way across India after photographing Gandhi, Nehru, famine victims and the Indian motion picture industry; Peter Gowland, who found an extraordinary nude model for me to photograph playing table tennis with author Henry Miller. There are others that come to mind: Ike Vern, Ruth Orkin, Ewing Krainin, Philippe Halsman, George Karger, Arthur Rothstein, André Kertész, Bob and Cornell Capa and W. Eugene Smith—it is from these men and women that I learned what I know about photography.

DON'T FORGET LIST

Don't forget list, which could also be called an *idiot list,* or *you can screw up your pictures if you do not pay attention to this list!*

1. Take the lens cap off your lens before taking the picture—unless you want a blank.

2. Be careful to keep the flap of your carrying case and/or your camera strap from hanging in front of the lens. This has ruined many pictures.

3. Keep your fingers well away from the front of the lens.

4. Be sure to use the right film at the right time: daylight type for daylight exposures, tungsten type for tungsten exposures; be equally careful about black and white film—slow, medium or fast.

5. You must know which film is in the camera. So, when you load it, tear off a portion of the film box (with the ASA speed or the exposure data) and put it in the slot on the back of your camera, if it has one. If not, tape it to the inside of your camera case or the back of your camera.

6. When you load your camera don't try for one extra exposure. See that both the top and bottom sprockets are engaged in the film winding mechanism.

7. Check the tension on the rewind knob and be sure that it turns when you expose the film leader.

8. Always load and unload your film out of the sunlight and away from bright spotlights.

9. Always use a lens shade.

10. Press the shutter release button gently. Do not jar or jerk it.

11. When making the exposure, remember how x-ray technicians work: inhale, hold your breath, press the shutter release—now breathe.

12. Triple brace your camera with your right hand, your left hand and your face.

13. Keep your camera cool and dry.

14. Keep your film cool and dry.

15. Keep yourself cool and dry.

16. Keep your lens clean by using lens tissue.

17. If you remove partly exposed film from your camera, put it in a light-proof container and mark the container with the type of film and the number of exposures. Skip at least two frames beyond the exposed film when you put it back into the camera and be sure you have your lens cap on when you wind off your exposed frames.

18. If you're not sure you have enough depth of field, step the aperture down and use a slower shutter speed.

19. Pre-crop your pictures in the viewfinder by getting closer to, or farther away from, your subject.

20. Change camera angles to lower or higher, rather than eye level, to improve the composition of some pictures.

21. Move your subject or yourself to eliminate trees, vines, signs, pictures and other extraneous objects in the background that may appear to be growing out of your subject's head. Keep your portrait background simple and uncluttered.

22. Make use of overcast skies, open shade, cloudy and even stormy days for good pictures in black and white and color. On sunny days use side-lighting and backlighting.

23. If your camera is automatic, check the battery or batteries often. Clean your flash contacts and check your flash batteries regularly.

24. Keep your own shadow out of the picture.

25. Be sure to take the correction filter (should you be using one) off when you change from one type of film to another.

26. Do not use electronic flash at a higher shutter speed than that recommended for your camera.

FILM INDEX

MONOCHROME FILMS (BLACK AND WHITE)

SLOW

Name	ASA (daylight)	ASA (tungsten)	Size
Vte Ultra	25	25	135, 120, Minolta 16, Minox
Kodak Panatomic-X	32	32	135, 120
Ilford Pan F	50	50	135

MEDIUM

Name	ASA (daylight)	ASA (tungsten)	Size
Fujipan K	125	125	126
Vte Ultra	80	80	135, 120, Minolta 16, Minox
Ilford FP4	125	125	135, 120, 127, 620
Kodak Verichrome Pan	125	125	110, 120, 126, 127
Kodak Plus-X Pan	125	125	135, 120

FAST

Name	ASA (daylight)	ASA (tungsten)	Size
Neopan SSS	200	200	135, 120
Ilford HP4	400	400	135, 120
Kodak Tri-X Pan	400	400	135, 120, 126, 127, 620
Ilford HP5	400	400	135, 120
Kodak 2475 Recording	NA	1000-3200	135-36
Kodak HIE 135 High Speed Infra Red	50 w/25A Filter		135
Kodak HC 135 (High Contrast)	Speed Varies with Development		135

INSTANT PICTURE MONOCHROME FILMS

MEDIUM (Positive-Negative)

Name	Exposures	ASA	Size
Polaroid 55 P/N	single	50	4 x 5 inches
665 P/N	single	50	3¼ x 4¼

FAST

Name	Exposures	ASA	Size
Pack 107	8	3000	3¼ x 4¼ inches
51	single	200	4 x 5 inches
52	single	400	4 x 5 inches
57	single	3000	4 x 5 inches
42	8	200	3¼ x 4¼ inches
47	8	3000	3¼ x 4¼ inches
46-L	8	800	2½ x 3¼ inches
Type 87	8	3000	3¼ x3¼ inches

DAYLIGHT COLOR FILMS

FOR TRANSPARENCIES (SLIDES, REVERSAL FILMS)

(Prints can be made from transparencies by means of a low-cost internegative.)

SLOW

Name	ASA	Size
Kodak Photo Micrography Film 2483	16	135-136 long rolls
Kodachrome 25	25	135

MEDIUM

Agfachrome 64	64	135, 120, 126, Rapid
Fujichrome RK	64	126
Fujichrome R100	100	135
Kodachrome 64	64	135, 110
Ektachrome 64	64	135
3M Color Slide	50	126, 135

FAST

CS (GAF)	200	135
GS (GAF)	500	135
Kodak 135 Ektachrome	200	135
Kodak 135 Ektachrome	160 Tungsten	135
Kodak Professional Ektachrome		
EPR 135	64	135
EPD 135	200	135
EPR 120	64	120
EPD 120	200	120
E6 Dupe	Dependent on Development	135
Kodak IE 135 Infra Red Color	Approx. 50 w/ No. 15 filter	135

FOR PRINTS (NEGATIVE FILMS)

MEDIUM

Name	ASA	Size
Agfacolor CNS	80	135, 120
Fujicolor NK	100	126
Fujicolor N 100	100	135, 120
Kodacolor II	100	110, 135, 126, 120 (CK)
Kodak Vericolor S	100	120, 220, 135
3M Color Print	80	126, 135
Sakura Color Print	80	126, 135

FAST

Fujicolor 400	400	135
Kodacolor 400	400	110, 135
Vericolor L	100T	120
Sakuracolor 400	400	135
3M-400	400	135

INSTANT PICTURE COLOR FILM

Name	Exposures	Picture Size
Polaroid Pack 108	8	3¼ x 4¼ inches
Pack # 620/108	8	3¼ x 4¼ inches
Pack # 636/108	8	3¼ x 4¼ inches
58	single	4 x 5 inches
48	6	3¼ x 4¼ inches
SX70	10	3½ x 3½ inches
88	8	3¼ x 3¼ inches
Kodak PR 10 Instant Print Film	10	2⅝ x 3‰16 inches

TUNGSTEN COLOR FILMS (3200K)

FOR TRANSPARENCIES (SLIDES, REVERSAL FILMS)

SLOW

Name	ASA	Size
Kodak Ekta Prof Type B	32	120, 4x5, 8x10

MEDIUM

	ASA	Size
EPY 135	50	135, 120

FAST

	ASA	Size
EPT	160	135, 120

(Prints can be made from transparencies by means of a low-cost internegative.)

TUNGSTEN COLOR FILMS (3400K)

FOR TRANSPARENCIES (SLIDES, REVERSAL FILMS)

SLOW

Name	ASA	Size
Kodachrome II (Type A)	40	135-36

(Prints can be made from transparencies by means of a low-cost internegative.)

GLOSSARY

Angle:
Your point of view or camera angle.

Aperture:
Lens opening which can be opened and closed. (Example: From small opening f/16 to large opening f/2. The larger the number the lesser amount of light transmitted.)

ASA:
Film emulsion speed standards set by the American Standards Association. (Example: ASA 100. The higher the number the more sensitive the film.)

Available light:
Means just that—no light added.

Backlight:
Light coming from behind the subject.

Bayonet mount:
A push-in, half-turn, lens mount (recommended).

Bounce light:
Created by turning flash or floodlight source to the wall or ceiling for softer overall light.

Bracketing:
Shooting three exposures—one that you think is the right one, one at a stop over and another at a stop under—just in case you're wrong.

Cartridge:
Case in which roll film is contained.

Cassette:
Metal holder for self-loading 35mm film when film is purchased in bulk.

CDS:
Cadmium sulphide light-sensitive cell used in many automatic camera exposure-metering systems. Also used in commercial exposure meters.

Composition:
The way you see and arrange the elements of the picture in the viewfinder.

Contact print:
The negative is placed in direct contact with the printing paper and exposed to light. Result is a same-size contact print.

Crop:
To trim or edit prints.

Crop marks:
Show indicated area to be printed. Can be used on contact or small prints to show how final enlargement should look.

Crosslight:
Two light sources, one on each side, cross one another on the subject.

Definition:
A relative term which can be used to describe the quality of sharpness and grain in a negative transparency or print.

Depth of field:
Defines the portion of the picture in sharp focus; that is, the distance between the sharpest point in the foreground to the sharpest point in the background.

Diaphragm:
The mechanism which opens and closes the aperture based upon the f stop.

Diapositive:
A word, usually used in Europe, to describe a color transparency.

Direct positive:
A no-negative film, such as Polaroid, or any self-developing film.

Dodge:
To expose more (or less) of a portion of a negative when making enlargements.

Double, triple or multiple exposure:
More than one exposure made on one negative or sheet or print paper.

Electronic flash:
A bright spark of light that is discharged when stored energy is released within a flash tube. Light is cool, of short duration and energy can be stored for many flashes.

186

Emulsion:
　The sensitized coating on photographic films and printing papers.

Exposure:
　Control of light by means of the camera lens opening and the shutter speed.

Exposure counter:
　Window indicator showing number of pictures taken or that remain to be taken.

Exposure meter:
　An instrument for measuring light density. Can be used to determine incident or reflected light.

Fill light:
　A light (flash, flood or reflector) used to lighten shadow areas, usually in portraiture.

Film speed:
　See ASA.

Filter factor:
　The amount of time that the exposure must be increased when using a filter. (Example: 2X equals one stop.)

Flash guide number:
　A variable number used for determining exposure depending upon type and speed of film, type of flashbulb or electronic flash.

Focal length:
　Used in reference to lenses, the focal length reveals the size of the image as well as its sharpness. (Example: Assuming that all pictures are taken with a 35mm camera from the same spot, a 21mm focal length wide angle lens will make the object small; a 50mm normal lens gives approximately human eye coverage; a 200mm telephoto lens produces a large image.

Fog:
　Light can leak into the film cartridge causing fog along the edges of the negatives. It is important to shade the film with your body when loading outdoors.

Fog filter:
　Piece of optically flat glass fitted to the lens to diffuse light. They come in different densities and can be used for either black and white or color photography. They are designated by a number; the higher the number the softer the picture.

Grain:

The texture of film; either color or monochromatic. Generally, fast films have coarser texture than slow films. In black and white processing, fine grain development yields less contrast but greater tonal values.

High-key:

A photograph with no dark tones and little or no contrast is known as a high-key picture. A technique often used in nude and fashion photography.

Incident light:

The light that strikes the subject as opposed to that which is reflected from it. Incident light meter readings are taken from the subject with the meter facing the camera.

Infinity:

When focusing the camera a point beyond which all will be in sharp focus.

Kelvin:

A thermometric scale used to indicate the color temperature of various light sources. (Example: tungsten floodlights 3200K; photofloods 3400K.)

Latitude:

The amount of exposure variation that a film allows while still producing a usable or acceptable print or transparency.

Lens cap:

Protective cover which fits over the lens.

Lens shade:

Fits over, and extends out from, the lens to reduce glare and extraneous light. Especially important when using backlight but always recommended.

Low-key:

Heavy shadows in overall dark print or transparency. Few highlights.

Macro lens:

Sometimes called micro because they are used for extreme closeup photography. Makes possible extreme close-ups without accessory lenses or extension tubes.

Motor drive:

Auxiliary motor that can be attached to some new automatic cameras. Automatically advances film, cocks shutter and rewinds film for removal from camera.

Normal lens:
On a 35mm camera this is a 50mm or a 55mm lens. The angle of view corresponds approximately with that of the human eye.

Open flash:
Used when no synchronization is available. Open the shutter, flash the bulb, close the shutter. Can only be used at low light levels.

Oxidation:
Deterioration of film or processing chemicals due to too long exposure to air, especially warm moist air.

Panchromatic film:
A film emulsion sensitive to all light colors. Represents most black and white film in use.

Panning:
Moving the camera along with the motion of the subject while releasing the shutter. Because camera and subject are moving at the same speed, subject is sharp, background is streaked by movement.

Parallax:
When the view from the viewfinder differs from that seen by the lens. Especially noticeable in close-ups.

Photomontage:
Multiple images which can be made in the camera on one negative or transparency or a series of different prints pasted into single picture.

Polarize:
To affect light by means of a special filter so that its vibrations are confined to a single plane. Polarizing filters can therefore reduce most atmospheric haze and eliminate most reflections.

Reticulation:
A breakup in the film emulsion sometimes causing multiple dots or small depressions. Can be produced by film being stored at very high temperatures, such as in a closed car or glove compartment in summertime or a camera left too long in the sun. Also sometimes caused in black and white processing using too-warm solutions.

Screw mount:
Lenses that are not bayonet mounts, as described earlier, are screw mounts. They screw directly into the camera.

Strobe:
Used (erroneously) to describe any electronic flash. Scientifically, an electronic tube is "strobed" when repetitively flashed.

Sub-miniature, pocket-size:
A camera using film smaller than 35mm.

Synchronization:
A within-the-camera contact that fires flash equipment (electronic, bulbs, cubes or bars) while the shutter is open. Plug in contact marked "X" for electronic flash, "M" for most other flash equipment.

Telephoto:
Acts like a telescope. Telephoto lenses enlarge distant objects by bringing them closer.

Time (and bulb) exposure:
Made by setting the shutter on "T" or "B" and opening it to expose the film. Usually used in dim light or to obtain great depth.

Tripod:
An adjustable stand with three legs and a rotating tilt top (usually detachable) to which the camera can be attached and kept motionless during an exposure.

Tungsten light:
Most artificial light including quartz, spot and floodlight but excluding fluorescent tubes.

Ultraviolet (UV) filter:
A flat piece of optical glass that absorbs ultraviolet rays. Also called haze filter.

Umbrella reflector:
Made of highly reflective material that reflects light back onto the subject. Looks like an umbrella.

Unipod:
A one-legged adjustable camera stand. Easy to carry, useful to steady the camera.

Wide angle lens:
A lens that takes in more area than the normal eye can see. The image size is smaller than that of the normal lens. Extreme (and effective) distortion results when this lens is tilted.

Zoom lenses:
After focusing, the zoom lens can be moved forward or back to increase the focal length of the lens from wide angle to normal to telephoto and to any focal length in between.

INDEX

H

I

K

L

SELECTED BIBLIOGRAPHY

Aspden, Ralph L., *Electronic Flash Photography.* New York: The Macmillan Company, 1960.

Bourke-White, Margaret, *You Have Seen Their Faces.* (text by E. Caldwell), 1937.

Clark, Kenneth, *Looking at Pictures.* New York: Holt, Rinehart and Winston, 1961.

Doty, R., *Photo-Secession; Photography as a Fine Art.* Rochester, N.Y.: The George Eastman House, 1960.

Eder, J. M., *History of Photography.* New York: 1945.

Grimm, Tom, *The Basic Book of Photography.* New York: New American Library, 1974.

Halsman, Philippe, *Halsman Sight and Insight.* Garden City, N.Y.: Doubleday & Company, Inc., 1972.

Hicks, W., *Words and Pictures; An Introduction to Photo-journalism.* New York: 1966.

Horan, J. D., *Timothy O'Sullivan, America's Forgotten Photographer.* New York: 1966.

Lacey, P., *The History of the Nude in Photography,* 1964.

Moran, James Sterling, *The Classic Woman.* New York: Playboy Press, 1971.

Newhall, B., *The Daguerreotype in America.* New York: 1961.

————— *The History of Photography.* New York: The Museum of Modern Art, 1964.

_____ *Latent Image; The Discovery of Photography.* Garden City, N.Y.: 1967.

Ovenden, Graham and Robert Melville, *Victorian Children.* New York: St. Martin's Press Inc., 1972.

Riis, Jacob A., *How the Other Half Lives.* New York: 1890.

Rothstein, A., *Photojournalism.* New York: 1956.

Ruesch, Jurgen and Weldon Kees, *Nonverbal Communication.* Berkeley and Los Angeles: University of California Press, 1956.

Samuels, Mike, M.D. and Nancy Samuels, *Seeing with the Mind's Eye.* New York: Random House Inc. and Berkeley, California: The Bookworks, 1975.

Sargent, Walter, *The Enjoyment and Use of Color.* New York: Dover Publications, Inc., 1964.

Shepard, Harriett and Lenore Meyer, *Posing for the Camera.* New York: Hastings House, 1960.

Stieglitz, Alfred, *Camera Work,* an illustrated quarterly magazine devoted to photography, published and edited by Alfred Stieglitz, 1902-1917.

Sussman, Aaron, *The Amateur Photographer's Handbook.* New York: Thomas Y. Crowell Company, 1973.

Szarkowski, J., *The Photographer's Eye.* New York: 1966.

Weston, Edward, *The Daybooks of Edward Weston.* Rochester, N.Y. and New York, 1961-66 (2 vols.).

The text and headings are set in Times
Roman, a type that was commissioned by
The Times of London and supervised by
Stanley Morison in the year 1931. The type
was set by Intertype Fototronics System by
Central Graphics of San Diego, California.
Color separations are by Toppan Graphic
Art Center, Mountainside, New Jersey.
Printed in the USA by Kingsport Press.
Production by Gemini Smith Inc., La Jolla,
California.

Photographs by Bradley Smith
Graphics: Sally Collins
Copy editor: Michael Smith
Manuscript preparation: Florence Kronfeld

My thanks to the following manufacturers
for the use of new camera equipment and
assistance with the latest technical data:

Canon Inc., Eastman Kodak Company,
Honeywell Photographic, Konica Camera
Company, Nikon Inc., Olympus Camera
Company, Polaroid Company.

   All of the new automatic cameras tested
out well as did Kodak's new Trimlite
Instamatic cameras.